Launching
Into the Unknown

The Beautiful and Bewildering World
of the Sudanese

Leoma Gilley

Edited and Proofed by Erin Tackitt
Cover Design by: Kristina Edstrom

PEAK PRESS

An Imprint for GracePoint Publishing (www.GracePointPublishing.*com)*

GracePoint Matrix, LLC
624 S. Cascade Ave, Suite 201
Colorado Springs, CO 80903
www.GracePointMatrix.com
Email: Admin@GracePointMatrix.com

SAN # 991-6032

Library of Congress Control Number: 2023941552

ISBN: (Paperback) 978-1-955272-95-7
eISBN: 978-1-955272-96-4

Books may be purchased for educational, business, or sales promotional use.
For bulk order requests and price schedule contact:
Orders@GracePointPublishing.com

Dedication

To the Sudanese people who showed me such gracious hospitality and patience. May peace come to your nation in our lifetime.

Table of Contents

Preface and Acknowledgements

"How do you find Sudan?" was one of the most common questions asked during my twenty-two years there. We want to know what others think of us, and we hope that the answer will be positive. My response to this question from the beginning has been, "The country is very difficult, but the people are very nice." So often for the Sudanese, the reports about them have been critical and harsh, equating the people of the Sudan with their government's policies.

This compilation of stories attempts to convey what life is like for the ordinary Sudanese. In the West, I'm asked, "How is Sudan different from here?" I wonder where to begin, since there are so few similarities. I find it hard to conceptualize the West and Sudan in my mind simultaneously, as if it weren't possible for both to be part of the same planet. And yet their dreams and aspirations in life are not so different.

Learning another culture is like walking around in the dark in an unfamiliar house. You don't know where anything is until you bump into it, sometimes gently, sometimes painfully. Meanwhile, you are desperately looking for a light switch, hoping to be able to see more clearly how to get around. One motivation for this book is to bring a little light and understanding about the world of the Sudanese.

They have learned to live in conditions far more challenging than anything I could have imagined. They have kept a wonderful outlook on life, and from them, I have learned some secrets to contentment that do not lie in the possession of things. While many of the people have relatively few possessions, they enjoy life and grasp it with passion. It is my Western assumptions that most often account for my frustrations and confusions. Perhaps as we come to "know ourselves better," as the Sudanese say, we will learn to respect and appreciate each other more.

I have sought to show each individual mentioned by name what I wrote about him or her before publication. Where that was not possible or where the person requested it, I changed the name to avoid embarrassment. I ask forgiveness in advance for any who are offended by my remarks. After all, I'm usually bumping around in the Sudanese world, still in the dark.

I want to thank Harriet Howell (the Harriet to whom I addressed the letters) as the only family member ever to visit me in Sudan. She inspired me to write a book. Thanks also go to Nancy Bowman for reading and commenting on the draft copies. I also owe a great debt of gratitude to Peter Mojwok, Prof. al-Amin Abumanga and Dr. al-Sadiq Yahya Izza for reading the material related to the Shilluk people (Peter) and the university (Prof. al-Amin and Dr. al-Sadiq), and checking with many other people for permission to use their names, photos, etc. This book would not have been possible without their help.

Chapter 1
At Home

Dear Harriet,

As my first cousin, you are the closest thing I have to a sister since I'm an only child. You did your best to make up for the brothers and sisters I didn't have. My home on the lake ensured I loved swimming, but there were no other children in the neighborhood. That made our relationship even more important.

It's fun to recall those times we had summer vacations in Florida together, especially when my parents decided the four of us would go from Chattanooga to Florida in a Volkswagen Beetle. We had our portraits done in chalk, and to get them home, Dad taped one to the inside roof of the car and the other inside the front hood. Even the mighty rainstorm we traveled through didn't harm them. I remember our time on Jekyll Island, also known as "Blaadom." Driving the go-carts proved the most eventful time for me, especially nearly running you down before crashing into the side rail. Those were wonderful days.

Now I'm starting on a new adventure. It began on a Wednesday evening at First Presbyterian Church in Chattanooga. We had a Wednesday night potluck dinner for fellowship and a short sermon. "What do you do for a living?" someone at my table asked.

"I'm a speech therapist."

"Oh, you mean like phonetics and stuff?" he asked.

"Yes."

"Well, then you might be interested in Wycliffe."

Never having heard of Wycliffe, I replied, "What's Wycliffe?"

"They do Bible translation with linguistics and stuff. They're making a presentation this weekend. You should go."

I attended, and the rest is history. I marveled at the idea of working with a small group of people, learning their language and culture, and helping translate the Bible. The presenter did a monolingual demonstration where he spoke a language none of us knew and, by using motions and objects, learned words from the speaker of another language. It fascinated me, and with my linguistic background, I worked out how he did it. Then I believe God put into my heart, "This is what I want you to do."

After much thought and prayer, I applied, but I received no response from the organization. So, I moved on to the next stage of my life, going to graduate school. After completing my M.A. in speech and language pathology, I took a job at a speech and hearing center in Macon, Georgia. First Presbyterian Church in Macon became my home church. I became part of an active singles' group and learned many important lessons both for life and for my spiritual development.

The call to join Wycliffe came to mind once more. As I considered applying again, I talked with my pastor. "How do I know if I'm called to do something?"

He suggested three ways: 1) You can't imagine doing anything else. 2) Others see you fitting that role of being in full-time ministry. 3) You know in your spirit that this is what you need to do.

Within weeks, several members of my singles' group commented to me, "I can see you as a missionary!" I had not mentioned considering such a career, so my response was, "You can?!"

To make a long story short, I applied again, and this time I got a response.

Love,

L

————————

Dear Harriet,

The lengthy application took me some time to complete. There was a theological section with questions like: What do you believe about the Bible? How do you understand the end times? I tried to explain them with what knowledge I had, but not having been to Bible college, I had limited understanding of several points. I asked the pastor who oversaw our singles' group for help. He had finished seminary a few years before. He gave me lots of books to read, and as I finished one, we would discuss it. After a few months, I was ready to send in my responses.

Upon receipt of my application, they sent questionnaires to people I had listed to assess my character. My neighbor was one of those, so I got to see what they wanted to know. The form asked how neatly I took care of my home, how I related to members of the opposite sex, and how I handled my finances. I can't imagine they could ask such personal questions these days, but back in 1978 they could, and did. We had a good laugh about it. She even shared the questions with some of her students at the school where she taught. They all agreed they didn't want anyone answering such personal questions about them.

One concern I had about this career was how I would react to a new environment. A few years before, I had almost died after having allergy tests for pollen. I had allergic reactions to everything that produces pollen. I recall the doctor telling me, "Try not to breathe except in January and February." He said this as he sought to control my systemic reaction to the tests. So, I wanted to get a second opinion from a specialist.

Mom and I consulted an allergy doctor in Atlanta, where they gave me a series of tests over a couple of days. Each time they injected small doses of food, dander, dust, and mold into my back, the nurse would say, "Don't scratch!" It never itched, so when she returned and began calling out my score for each thing, I was surprised. The scale is 1-4, with 1 being very little reaction and 4 being a significant reaction. She would call out, 2, 4, 4, 3, 4, 3, 3, 1, 4, 4, 4, etc. My allergies were more serious than I had thought.

The last series of tests were the pollens. I explained to them what had happened before and cautioned each nurse, "Don't kill me. My mother is here and she won't like that!" Pop, pop, pop went the injections and the caution, "Don't scratch!" Within moments, my back felt as though a million ants were chewing on me. I got up to check my back in the mirror and saw welts several inches across. (A score of 4 meant the welt was the size of a quarter.) The nurse nearby heard me moving around, and again said, "Don't scratch!"

"If you hear me screaming, you'll know I'm not scratching."

In a few minutes, she came in to check on me. "Oh, you did have a reaction." That began a parade of all the staff to have a look at my back. But to their credit, they didn't kill me.

When I returned to get the doctor's report, it didn't put my mind at ease. He noted I had "immense allergies." He said it had disturbed him when my first battery of tests came out, but when we got to the pollen, "You took the roof off the building!"

"What does this mean for working in a location without air conditioning?"

"Oh, it probably won't matter," he replied.

"What do you mean?"

"Wherever you go, you'll become allergic to whatever is there."

I began a regime of allergy shots. They gave me three vials to use. The first contained trees and grass, the second, weeds and the third included everything else. He gave me instructions to test for food allergies. Throughout my training, I took the shots. The 'everything' bottle proceeded normally. However, the pollen bottles had to be monitored closely. Instead of increasing from 0.5 ml to 1.0 ml, etc., I could only move from 0.01 to 0.02 about every two weeks. A nurse gave the injections and then watched to ensure I didn't have a serious reaction.

Love,

L

————

Dear Harriet,

The next stage of the process required me to attend the SIL course in Dallas, Texas. In August 1979, I quit my job, packed up my car, and headed to Dallas. At the SIL center, I moved into a dorm room with a small kitchenette. That provided a way for me to monitor my diet more closely, as I still needed to do the food allergy test. My roommate hailed from New York.

As we rearranged the furniture, I strained my back. Before classes began, my back problem became so severe that I couldn't get out of bed. The nurse called in an osteopath. He manipulated my back to get it unstuck and told me to stay in bed for several days. My poor roommate was on bedpan duty! Neither of us had signed up for that. The one time I tried to make it to the bathroom, the pain was so intense I ended up on the floor.

Then it rained, and I discovered we had a hole in our roof and ceiling. We put a bucket next to my bed to catch the water, but the drip, drip, drip was annoying and torturous. Someone came up with the brilliant idea of tying a long piece of string to a cotton ball. They stuffed the cotton ball into the hole in the ceiling and ran the string into the bucket. That way, the water ran down the string without the constant drip.

While my colleagues attended class, I lay in bed watching a grasshopper. Our room was on the upper floor, but this grass-hopper climbed up to our balcony almost every day. He had part of a leg missing, so I'm sure it was the same one.

My fellow students returned each day with assignments for me. I asked if they understood phonetics. I taught them what they didn't understand. After a week, I attended class. However, my movements were very limited. I could just get one foot slightly in front of the other. So, while everyone else got acquainted, I stayed alone in my room or lying on the floor of the classroom. It was not possible to sit for more than about 30 minutes.

At last, I improved enough to attend classes and eat in the dining hall. As soon as I ate something I was allergic to, my body would tell me. One of those items turned out to be the syrup for pancakes. I don't know what it contained, but it did not like me.

Despite these setbacks, I made some wonderful friends and did well on the course. Linguistics turned out to be my thing.

We took a test of our Bible knowledge and all those years in Sunday School helped me correctly answer most of the questions. They also interviewed each person extensively. At the end, they told me the divorce in my past would not prevent me from membership. That was a relief. In fact, the interviewer gave me a scripture that remains precious to me. "I (the LORD) will repay you for the years the locusts have eaten" (Joel 2:25a, NIV).

At the end of the term, a letter from Wycliffe appeared in my mailbox. They accepted me. Now the reality set in.

Love,

L

———

Dear Harriet,

I still needed to complete two more semesters of training, so after the Christmas break, I took the second semester, adding M.A. credit from the University of Texas at Arlington to my resume. Norman, Oklahoma was the original home for the SIL school, so the training in Dallas returned there in the summers. I spent the summer there and came down with shingles. In 1980, the only treatment was morphine, but it made little difference. It felt like a hot iron sitting on my skin. The only relief was ice. So, I lived with ice as my best friend for a couple of weeks. Going to class became a challenge since anything that touched the blisters made them hurt all the more. It was NOT a pleasant experience.

At the end of the term, I came down with a virus that caused severe nausea. I couldn't eat and barely drank anything. Some friends took me and my car to Dallas, where I stayed with other friends from church. They took me to the hospital, where an IV drip got me back to my normal state.

In between terms, I met with another mission organization affiliated with the Presbyterian Church. Even though I went to a Baptist church in college, I switched to a Presbyterian church and continued with that denomination. I needed access to churches in order to raise support, so having dual membership with Wycliffe and the Presbyterian mission board made that possible. During my interview with Mission to the World, they decided I should have counseling before leaving for an assignment abroad. Since Wycliffe/SIL offered counseling in Dallas, I elected to take a fourth semester of classes while fulfilling the counseling requirement.

I moved into a house with four other women, and we had a blast together. All of us were very different. We lived on Forest Lane and called ourselves the Forest Lane Singers, or the Four Slain Singers, if you said it quickly enough. On occasions, we sang together at the house and even in a chapel service. Most of our songs were Christian, but anything was possible at the house. The extra courses and the counseling went well, and at the end of that term, it was time to do some serious fundraising.

Love,

L

————

Dear Harriet,

For the next year, I visited various churches, mostly in the Southeast, speaking and sharing my vision for Bible translation. I decided I would not ask for money directly. If this was what God wanted me to do, then the funds would come in. I asked for prayer.

As my departure date of January 1982 approached, I began packing a large wooden crate with things that would be useful in my assignment. I bought a small gas oven with three burners on top. It was made for use in a mobile home, so it was quite compact. My uncle made two cedar chests for me with movable shelves. He also built cedar tables for them to sit on. I could use them to store items or as a desk or a kitchen cupboard. I bought clothes I hoped would be appropriate, kitchen items, and books. This crate was to be shipped by sea to Mombasa, Kenya.

To get in shape physically, I began walking up and down our country road each day. I added cans of vegetables and fruit to my backpack and walked farther each day until I easily walked four miles.

I visited some of my good friends to say my last farewells. While staying with a friend in Knoxville, I became concerned that all of this was a big mistake. *What was I thinking? I'm leaving everything and everyone to live on another continent. Why did I think I could do that? What if this was a mistake and I spent all that money and time to go and then just have to come home defeated?* Fear and anxiety took over.

At that point, I got out of bed and knelt on the floor. "God, if this is what you want me to do, I should not be this afraid. Tell me now if I'm headed in the wrong direction, so I don't waste all this money."

I waited. Then in my mind, I sensed God saying to me, "You are holding so tightly to the things you have that there is no room for me to give you anything new. Open your hands and allow me to take what I need to take, so there is room to give you what I want you to have." I opened my hands and found peace.

Each suitcase could only weigh a total of 44 lbs. because of the weight restrictions once I reached Europe. I planned to stop in England for a few days to say farewell to some friends there. I packed and repacked until I got it right. What I took in these cases had to last me for three months at least. I carefully evaluated every item.

On January 14, 1982, my parents, pastor, and family friends saw me off at the airport. Mom gave me a necklace with a gold disk with the date on one side and "Go with God" on the other. I was excited. My parents grieved, but no one cried in my presence. With a kiss, a hug, and a wave, my journey into the unknown had begun.

Love,

L

Chapter 2
Orientation: Learning to Adapt

Dear Harriet,

My first solo international flight was on KLM. Excited to start on this adventure, I wanted someone to talk with about it. A businessman sitting in business class invited me to join him. I chatted away and he seemed interested. As we landed in Amsterdam, I hurried back to my seat to collect my hand luggage. There was time, as the doors of the plane had frozen shut. I was so disorganized, I was the last one on the plane and the flight attendant was giving me questioning looks. I quickly realized I needed to keep better track of my possessions on a plane or I would leave bits behind regularly.

After a week in England visiting friends, it was time to depart for a warmer climate. England was experiencing one of the coldest winters on record. Bundled up in a coat, scarf, jeans, and boots, I made my way to Heathrow Airport for the initial flight to Amsterdam before heading to Cameroon. At check-in, I noticed another single woman whose backpack indicated the same arrival address tag as mine. I guessed correctly that Jill and I were both going to the capital of Cameroon, Yaoundé [YAWN day], for SIL's three-month orientation course to help us live successfully in Africa.

Jill planned to keep the books for the group in Sudan and live in the Southern Region's capital of Juba. Juba was and still is a rough-and-tumble place. Since my training prepared me for work on linguistics and literacy, I expected to live in a Kenyan village. The orientation course was to teach us to cook using local products and to avoid health hazards like amoeba, giardia, poisonous snakes, and dirty water. Hopefully, helping us learn how to function without modern conveniences and to understand our African neighbors would make our adjustment easier. This orientation in Cameroon served our organization's work in Africa.

After flying to Amsterdam, we met up with a family also headed to Cameroon, Keith and Ruth and their two boys, both under four years of age. The six of us made stopovers in Europe from the U.S. and Canada. Jill and I knew about the 20 kg rule, while Keith and Ruth did not.

In case you don't know, when you fly out of the U.S. or Canada, you can have 30 kg (55 lbs) in each of two suitcases per person. When you fly out of Europe, you can have 20 kg (44 lbs) per person. Since we stopped in Europe for over 24 hours, the 20 kg rule applied. Rather than pay overweight, Keith and Ruth repacked their suitcases in the airport and shipped their overweight on to Ghana, their eventual destination. We teamed up together and caught our flight to Paris, where things went seriously downhill.

To this day (forty years later and after thousands of miles traveled), our time in Charles de Gaulle Airport has remained my worst travel nightmare. Assuming we needed to stay in the international wing, since we were continuing on to Africa from Paris, we stayed put. Unfortunately, no restaurants or shops were to be found in this part of the terminal. There was, however, an area for mothers with small children, where Ruth stayed with the two boys. The rest of us prowled around for what seemed to be hours and decided we had to find some food. Because of this eventful trip, I learned to hoard any leftovers from the plane for just such times of imposed famine.

After searching, we discovered that if we went through immigration into France, we could get to shops and food! So, Keith, Jill, and I passed through immigration several times, with stamps entered into our passports each time, until we got to know the immigration officer quite well. The food was tolerable and expensive, but at least we had something to eat. We brought food in for Ruth and the boys. After spending most of the day crossing the border, finally it was time to board our flight to Africa.

Only then did we discover this flight from Paris stopped first in Marseilles, and thus we had to cross the border again for the domestic leg of the flight. Had we known, we could have spent the day in Paris instead of in the airport.

At this point, I learned the second valuable lesson of internat-ional travel: Make sure you can lift your hand luggage. My snazzy backpack rested on a set of wheels so I could pull it instead of carrying it. That worked pretty well in the U.S. and England, but in Paris they led us outside to walk around the terminal to our plane. Since we were on the tarmac and not inside the terminal, we had to carry hand baggage up the steps onto the plane. That's when I learned I needed stronger muscles or a lighter bag.

By this time, I had been traveling for nineteen hours. As soon as we took off from Paris, I was sound asleep. So, it was a rude awakening to be told in Marseilles to get off the plane to go through the immigration process yet again! After all, the last stamp in my passport read, "enter France!" Bleary-eyed, I shuffled out of the plane with Jill and Keith. Ruth was allowed to stay put because of the small boys. I coveted one of those children to claim as my own! Immigration stamped my passport, and I followed the other passengers back onboard, where I fell asleep again before we took off.

At some point, breakfast arrived, about twenty minutes after I fell asleep, or so it felt. By this time, I was so tired that I nearly got sick trying to eat. I decided that a quick trip to the little room for one of those private moments would help clear my head and sort out my stomach. Here I learned how important it is to drink a lot of fluids on a long flight. Dehydration is a terrible thing. Upon returning, I discovered the crew had removed my tray, and I had nothing to eat. My mistake was not asking for it back!

Within a short time, we landed at Douala, a coastal town on the Atlantic Ocean, the port of entry to Cameroon. Walking through the hallway to the terminal, I realized I was overdressed for the occasion. It must have been 90°F and 80 percent humidity. The airport was not air-conditioned, and so my suffering began. We met up with another family headed for orientation, Ken and Judy and their three girls. Ken played a significant part in the next segment of this adventure. As they were also going to work in Kenya, I immediately felt a kinship with them. By this time, our group comprised eleven people. Within a few hours, that number grew to fifteen as more people arrived to attend the same orientation.

We piled our gear and extra clothes and luggage into a large heap in the middle of the floor in front of the check-in desk, since we were several hours early for the flight from Douala to Yaoundé. With no seats in that area of the airport, some of us single folks stood guard over the baggage. The moms took the little ones to the one air-conditioned restaurant to drink very expensive sodas. Ken took up his position at the check-in desk to get everyone boarding passes. At the beginning, the agent told him none of our names were on the passenger list. That we had confirmed our seats seemed to carry no weight with the agent.

Love,

L

———————

Dear Harriet,

Ken had been a civil servant for some years in California and was a "people person." None of us knew much about Africans, but he had the good sense to stand at that desk and talk to that agent whenever he got a chance for the better part of four hours. The agent was from the English-speaking part of Cameroon, so communication was not a problem. Ken learned all about his family and how long he had worked there, and the agent learned we were in Cameroon to take a course and more. Finally, as other travelers got boarding cards for this flight and we did not, the agent said to Ken, "There are five people in your family?"

Ken answered, "Yes."

The agent said, "If you hold one child on your lap, I can get you on this flight."

Ken agreed and handed him their five tickets. In a few minutes, he got back the five tickets and four boarding passes. He thanked the agent, and then handed him the other ten tickets. The agent nearly fainted at this unspoken request, but because of the relationship established with Ken, he returned the tickets with ten boarding passes. We all hastened to the plane.

At this point, I learned another valuable lesson for traveling in Africa: Don't be the last person to board the plane! I held a boarding pass, but no seat! When this became clear, Ken's wife held another of their children in her lap for the one-hour flight so I could have the last seat.

With some relief, we settled in for what we hoped would be an uneventful trip. About midway to Yaoundé, the man sitting behind me had a sudden, urgent need for a cup of tea. He pulled out his charcoal stove and moved toward the aisle to light the charcoal to make his tea when the flight attendant saw him. He had imbibed rather too much of something else prior to getting on the flight and was not interested in alternatives. The captain hurried from the cockpit to explain in no uncertain terms that the man could have tea from the kitchen but could NOT make his own. I thought, *The FAA would not allow this, but they aren't here!* It was the first time I realized that the protection of laws, rules, and regulations that had governed my existence and safety up to that point no longer applied.

We landed without further excitement in Yaoundé, and our colleagues met us. We collected our baggage—at least most of us did. I learned yet another great lesson of international travel: Always carry a change of clothes in your hand luggage! None of the bags for Keith, Ruth, or their children arrived. The airline promised to trace their baggage and get it there as quickly as possible. In the meantime, they had almost nothing to wear and no special birthday cake mix for one child.

At the training center, everyone unpacked and picked out a few things for Ruth or Keith or the boys to wear. I handed over a dress or two, some underwear and handkerchiefs. It felt like a major sacrifice but, weeks later, after receiving their luggage, Ruth gave back my things. I hadn't even missed them. Another lesson learned: Make do with what you have.

By the time we arrived and settled in, exhaustion overtook me. I crashed onto the bed and fell asleep until someone woke me for supper. The only thing I had eaten was a bar of chocolate purchased in Amsterdam. After supper, I felt ready to return to my bed, but needed a shower. I collected my towel, soap, etc., and headed to the concrete-block bathhouse. When the sun sets in Africa, the temperature drops quickly. A cold shower is not the most pleasant of activities, but I was desperate, so I gritted my teeth and jumped in. It was brief, exhilarating, and it didn't prevent me from falling into a dreamless sleep on my first night in Africa.

Love,

L

———

Dear Harriet,

Having arrived in Africa, the time had come to begin my orientation, even though the challenges of arriving had started that process quite nicely! During our first three weeks, we attended classes on topics such as learning about local markets, speaking essential French, and cooking with local foods. There were lectures and demonstrations for cutting hair, carpentry, using a kerosene stove, coping with kerosene fridges, how to ride a motorcycle, and how to take care of a car. We attended several hours of class in the morning and more in the afternoon. Lectures also included basic health instruction and an introduction to books like *Where There Is No Doctor.*

That book has been a standard for years and, when I left Africa, I owned three copies.

Leoma and Karla learning
carpentry

Learning to take care of a kerosene
stove

Learning to care for a kerosene
refrigerator

The lecturers informed us about the local wildlife, the things we fear most, such as spiders, snakes, and scorpions. At one point a lecturer told us if we saw a black snake approximately six feet long in a tree, it was likely a black mamba (the "African two-step": You take two steps after it bites you and you're dead!). However, if it was under six feet long and black and on the ground, it might be a cobra. Cobras spit in your eyes to blind you before they bite you. The teacher presented all of this with a laissez-faire attitude, which I assume was designed to reduce our fear level. They kept saying the snakes feared us more than we feared them, but I reckoned there was more of me to be afraid, and that counted for something. Anyway, I couldn't resist the urge to ask if the snake minded very much being measured. The teacher suggested we kill it first.

One day, we ventured into town to the huge market. I am not much of a shopper, but the material was too wonderful to pass up. I bought several *pagnes* or *panyas*. *Panyas* are approximately six yards of material that I cut in half. One half I wrapped around me as a skirt. The other half served many possible purposes: tie a baby on one's back, or use as a basket, a sheet, a shawl, a tablecloth, or curtains. The bright colors last very well and look as bright now as on the day I bought the material. On the other hand, I found the meat market much less appealing, but I won't cover that topic!

The amount of food we received and the limited choices became big issues back at camp. Breakfast was comprised of uncooked oats, reconstituted powdered milk, bread, and chocolate spread. I choked down the oats and learned to love the chocolate spread. As I recall, bread and spreads were served for lunch, so everyone looked forward to a big supper. However, for the first week, the meager portions failed to satisfy. The leadership assigned us to teams to prepare meals and when my turn came to fix supper, I decided we would have enough food. One of the menu choices was papaya with ground beef. We baked half a papaya for each person and when we brought out the food, there was applause, especially from the men. For once, they had enough to eat.

At the end of the three weeks, we singles chose someone to live with and decided what supplies we would need in the coming five weeks of the training course's village phase. I teamed up with Betty, and between us we had no idea how much food would carry us through the end of February. From a list of available items, we filled out the quantities we wanted based firmly on guesswork.

Our tasks for this phase included learning to live in an African village, using our foodstuffs wisely, relating to the locals to learn their language, Ewondo, and writing a short anthropology paper. At least Betty spoke French, which was more than I was able to do. The leaders assigned us several books and articles to read. The village had no electricity or running water and the houses were constructed from mud bricks with tin or iron roofs. I got into the bush taxi, a twelve-seater van with at least fifteen people and a few animals, for the ride to our village, Mekomba.

Love

L

―――――――

Dear Harriet,

Glad you enjoyed the last installment. By the way, a papaya is a large fleshy fruit the size of an acorn squash. The inside is a lovely orange color and tastes very sweet. Papaya is sometimes used as a meat tenderizer. Huge spongy seeds fill the center. Those seeds always remind me of the frog eggs I saw when we dissected those six- to eight-inch-long frogs in biology class (ugh!). However, papaya seeds have many uses. If you can stand to eat them, they cure giardia and even amoeba problems. I am assured it does work, but never tried it myself. They taste bitter and are difficult to swallow, and then there is the "frog-egg-thought" to overcome. That is probably more than you wanted to know about papayas, so I shall return to my story.

To arrive at the village, I think we traveled about two hours by bush taxi, squashed in with lots of locals, who likely thought we were another crazy bunch of tourists looking for a cheap thrill. They weren't off by much.

Mekomba stretched over a half mile along the main dirt road. The houses were rectangular mud-brick constructions with zinc (metal) roofs. In most homes, they separated the kitchen from the house to prevent fires. Some of our host families moved into the kitchen to allow us the run of the house. The entire village consisted of fifty-six people, and there were twenty-six of us, so we significantly increased the population for the five weeks we spent there. Betty and I lived in the house of the village chief, across the square from the village president. We set up our camp beds and sorted out our possessions as best we could in our assigned room, given there were no closets, cupboards, dressers, or furniture of any kind, except maybe a chair or two. My camp bed suffered a major defect: In the middle of the night, it unhinged itself and left my lower half on the ground. Fortunately, after a night or two of this (and very little sleep), I exchanged it for one that stayed together.

We each used a mosquito net and learned to appreciate its many uses. At night, the mosquitoes came out in force, the nasty "malaria" kind and the not so nasty but much noisier "non-malaria" kind. If you can hear them, they won't kill you. It's the ones you can't hear that you must worry about. During the day, huge horsefly-like insects appeared that bit through one's clothes and hurt. They carried *filaria* or "river blindness." After the bite, the parasite grows and develops and finally, you go blind. There is still no cure. You can destroy the *filaria* before it gets to that stage but, as I understand it, they are very resistant to being poisoned and fight back in unpleasant ways. I don't think that any of us caught it.

(CAUTION: If you are squeamish, you may want to skip this paragraph.) The most aggravating insects, however, could not be kept out with a mosquito net—the jiggers. Now, I am familiar with chiggers from home, but they don't come close to jiggers! Jiggers live around pigs, and this village had pigs. Jiggers are tiny and black and love to burrow into the soft, fleshy part of your toes right near the toenail. They lay eggs and, before you know it, there is a huge white blister on your toe. It hurts because the egg sac takes up room, so you have to remove it. However, the sac is under the skin, so it is necessary to get a pin and open up the skin without breaking the egg sac. If you break the egg sac, you will spread the jiggers to even more parts of your foot. I have never been one to inflict pain on myself, so when I discovered jiggers had invaded my foot, I tried for a few minutes to deliver myself with a straight pin sterilized over a candle flame. The depth necessary to get under the sac was farther than I could will myself to go, so I called Françoise. She lived in our household and was about ten years old. Since she had practice getting jiggers out of her own feet, she was a marvel with mine. She became my "coping strategy" for this unpleasant task, which she repeated numerous times during my stay. Wearing closed-toe shoes and socks did not help, though putting citronella on my toes seemed to reduce the number of jiggers visiting me. The day I left Mekomba and returned to Yaoundé, I discovered one mama jigger had come with me. Françoise was no longer close at hand, and I had to deal with that one myself. It says a lot that I can still remember it!

Betty was my other coping strategy, since I spoke only about fifty words of French when we arrived. However, her stress level rose significantly upon discovering that French had become a tone language in this part of Africa. (A tone language allows differences in meaning with the change of pitch of one's voice. The sounds are the same, but the pitch changes.) Since French is not normally tonal, communication was rather more difficult than she had anticipated. Still, during that time we both tried to learn Ewondo. Betty achieved a bit more success because she spoke French to communicate what she wanted to learn. I used the less efficient monolingual approach and ended up learning more French, as that was the easier of the two languages. But when I tried to speak in French with the family and others in the village, they refused to use it since they knew who among us really spoke French and who didn't. I was in the latter category, so they spoke to me in Ewondo. I was pretty much in the dark most of the time.

Love,

L

Dear Harriet,

During our stay in Mekomba, some people became sick, and I was one of them. Many got malaria, but I got dengue fever! Its nickname is "break-bone fever" and that is how it feels. I hurt all the way into my bones, unable to do more than lie on my bed. It took about ten days before I regained much strength. During that illness, I changed households, as having a sick teammate required too much from Betty. I moved into a household with three others: Jill, Jan, and Karla.

One of my brilliant observations during this time was, "When the sun goes down, it is dark!" Now that may seem obvious, but having lived with electricity all of my life, I didn't realize how dark night could be. The night skies were glorious to behold, and it was a joy to sit outside and enjoy the view. Inside, it was another matter. While our mud floor appeared to be flat and smooth during the day, it became like an undulating wave at night, one that proved rather tricky to walk across, especially as I carried the remains of dishwashing water to the back door. Have you ever tried to carry a large, shallow basin half full of water across an uneven floor in the dark while also trying to hold a flashlight with your elbow?

Then there was the matter of taking a shower. When we arrived, there was fear that the water source might be infested with *bilharzia*, nasty flatworms that live in water. When you get the water on your skin, a worm in the water bores through the skin and enters the new host: You! It lives for a time in your liver while reproducing itself, causing fever and various skin problems. The offspring then enter the urinary tract, and if the infected person follows an all-too-common practice of urinating in a pool of water, the contamination continues.

We wanted to avoid any contact with infected water, so for the first few days of our stay we drank, washed, and cooked with the water we brought with us. Did you ever think you could feel refreshed after washing in half a mug of water?

After two days, tests showed the water to be free of *bilharzia* and we could use the local water source more freely. We had buckets and a large basin with which to do all water-related activities. There was no running water in any houses in the village. Each morning and afternoon, we took our buckets to the spring, filled them, and carried them back to the house. Carrying two buckets of water requires strength, and toting only one bucket required shifting it from hand to hand. I soon learned that carrying the bucket on my head held distinct advantages. It equalized the weight, and if it spilled, I felt cooler.

The instructors during our orientation encouraged us to wear a hat when walking through the forest. That way, when one of those six-foot-long snakes dropped out of a tree onto us, it might hit the hat and bite that instead of getting us—what a wonderful possibility! My hat was made of soft cotton and I don't believe it would have slowed down a determined black mamba. Fortunately, that situation never arose. Hats also protect from sunstroke in the intense sunlight.

In the middle of one night, the sound of the household's African members rushing around throwing water on the floor woke me up. I wasn't sure what they were doing. Should I get up and join them or stay safely in bed? Jan sat up and I asked what she thought was going on. She didn't answer and later had no recollection of anything. I'm sorry to say I stayed in bed. In the morning, we asked what happened. They looked weary and informed us that army ants had invaded the house and they fought them off with water and kerosene. Army ants can kill a small child. They will eat every bug or uncovered scrap of food in the place. If you meet them on a forest path, let them have the right of way and get out of there as quickly as your two legs will carry you.

The women of our village worked in gardens near the house. They cultivated cassava and other vegetables. We went along once or twice, but since none of us knew how to perform any of the required tasks, we tended to stay home and finish our reading assignments. They must have thought us quite lazy.

Our village family: Françoise is second from the right, front row

Early on during the orientation course, we discovered Karla had captured the heart of the most eligible single man on the staff. We watched the further development of their relationship with some interest. Jan and I considered working together, so it seemed most appropriate that we should try living in the same house during the rest of our training. In the end, we decided not to team up, but I enjoyed getting to know her.

Jill, whom I had met at the airport in England, came to work as a bookkeeper. She saw no need to learn a new language and culture, so she volunteered to be our household's chef while we did our anthropology research and language learning. One day, she made a batch of no-bake cookies: oats mixed with butter, sugar, and chocolate. Very nice! We immediately ate one or two when we got home in the evening. When we offered one to Jill, she confessed she had made a batch but then had eaten all of them herself. Later she felt guilty, so she made another batch so we wouldn't know what she had done. Despite all that effort, she told us about it! Culture stress makes you do strange things.

There were two other major events in our training: a village visit and a jungle overnight. I'll tell you about them in my next letter.

Love,

L

───────

Dear Harriet,

Once we became somewhat used to living in Mekomba, the staff assigned us another village to visit overnight. We walked there, a jaunt of several miles, while carrying our stuff on our backs. The long walk would serve to get us physically fit. I suppose it did that, at least briefly. Jan had health issues that prevented her from walking very far, so she put her gear in a truck. I have to say I took advantage and gave her a few of my heavier things, which rode in the truck. Since our training aimed to teach us coping strategies, I decided I was applying what I had learned.

Our village hostess was busy making *baton d'manioc* to sell in the market. This is a stick of cassava wrapped in a banana leaf. She and other neighbor ladies pounded cassava into a powder, with great effort. (Give me a large blender and electricity to run it, please!) They boiled it in a large kettle over a charcoal fire until it became a stiff paste. They scooped the paste out of the large kettle onto a banana leaf. After folding the leaf around the paste, it looked like a one-inch-thick stick. The women steam the sticks in another enormous pot until cooked.

We helped with this work, or more accurately, we observed the cassava being processed. Afterward, we enjoyed the dubious pleasure of eating it for supper. After unwrapping the manioc from the banana leaf, we dipped the now rubberized cassava (manioc) into the stew or sauce. I compared the experience to what I imagine it is like to eat a gum eraser. When first produced, it was edible, but the next morning it had fermented and I couldn't choke it down. I slipped most of my manioc to the host family's dog, which was not as squeamish as I. The other new treat for the evening meal included palm wine. When first made, it tasted mild and contained enough alcohol content to decontaminate the water. As Jan handed me the orange plastic glass, she whispered, "I think it has little 'floaties' in it." I took a small sip and tried to sieve it through my teeth, smiled, and passed the palm wine along to the person on my right.

The daughters of the family took us "girls" to their local swimming hole for a bath. We followed their lead and disrobed and swam *au naturel*. The girls were quite curious to see if we were white all over. We provided plenty of gossip for the neighborhood for months after that. The girls posted a guard on the path in case young men happened by. They did. A warning whistle signaled us to go underwater with only our heads sticking out. Then the guys passed by, and when the all clear sounded, we resumed our swim. It was one of the most pleasant activities of our time in Cameroon.

There comes a time, actually several times in each day, when the call of nature comes to us all. In the village where we overnighted, there was one facility, a large pit with three or four shaky boards over it. When Ruth paid her call, she found that a baby goat had fallen into the pit below, and was bleating for help. The owner finally rescued the poor thing. Otherwise, what a horrible way to go.

In the village where we lived, there were two "facilities," one behind the president's house and one behind my first home. After a couple of visits to ours, I elected to cross the square to the president's. You may not want to ask why, but I shall tell you anyway. Our loo, as the British say, was on the edge of the forest, near a well-used path. So, as I perched precariously on the wobbly planks covering the large and fairly full pit, watching the maggots crawling around below me, I heard young men walking along the path and I realized I was not hidden from view. The president's facility had a concrete cover over the pit and a grass fence around it. Not everyone hit the hole, but at least I wasn't worried about falling in or being watched. Enough said about that!

Let me return to the village visit. After a night of feasting on manioc and new palm wine, our host felt hungover. We had not slept well and looked forward to a ride back to Mekomba as soon as possible. My emergency supply of granola was running low, as I supplemented my diet with that to make up for what I couldn't face at breakfast. As we waited for our ride, our host made conversation. He spoke in French, so Jan translated for me. He offered to marry me, giving me the opportunity to become his second, or possibly third, wife. This proposal stunned me to speechlessness, which is saying something for me. At first, it offended me that he considered making such an offer, but I recognized a negative attitude would not solve my dilemma. That's when I remembered advice we gained during orientation's initial three weeks. I explained my father had to give permission, and I didn't expect he would. Honor was satisfied. Our ride arrived, and we breathed a sigh of relief.

Love,

L

———

Dear Harriet,

Our jungle overnight proved no less exciting. While we planned our village visit, the jungle overnight was supposed to be a surprise. The rationale for this venture was to prepare us in the event a catastrophe overtook us, forcing us to live in the bush. I've never needed this skill, but if the occasion arises, I'm trained! Since my teammate Jan had problems walking, we knew when our turn was coming, and we camped at a location closer to Mekomba. So, on that fateful day, we gathered our things and met our leaders. We grabbed our backpacks loaded with a *panga* (a knife with an eighteen-inch blade for cutting our way through the forest), a pot, matches, a length of rope, a blanket, extra clothes and the ever-present granola with powdered milk mixed into it. As we lined up for the trek, each of us received a live chicken. Why someone would evacuate with a live chicken is anyone's guess, but the mystique of "jungle camp" was that you had to kill a chicken.

Off we started in single file to our campsite, about a half hour away from the village. Upon arrival, we split up, each person for himself or herself. I believe they let families stay together. We were supposed to cut two or three trees to make a platform. The tree trunks were to be tied together with strips of palm branches. Palm branches proved to have multiple uses, as one could cut and strip the leaves from the plant and then shave the stalk, producing strong twine-like material. Having done that, we used the rope and palm branches to weave a bed. More palm branches covered the woven structure. My bed was high off the ground, so I had no worries about creepy crawlies. At that point, we built a fire. Plenty of fuel was available in the forest.

I was still recovering from dengue fever when I did this, so when my panga hit an ironwood tree, the clanging sound informed me I had chosen the WRONG tree! It might look small, but it would defeat me. By the time I completed my chopping, splitting, tying, and weaving, it was nearly dark. I built my campfire and thanked God and my parents for those years I attended summer camp and learned how to do such things. Supper consisted of my granola with powdered milk—just add water and my meal was ready! Using a long stick, I managed my fire from the safety of my bed and prepared to enjoy the fruit of my labor.

One staff member came by and seemed surprised to find me comfortably ensconced on my bed. He probably thought of me as a wimp—though he did not use that word—and expected me to be at my wit's end. Little did he know I was made of sterner stuff.

In the morning, I ate more of my granola and joyfully prepared to depart for an early appointment in the village. Jan and I were talking to the director regarding various issues, so we left ahead of the others. I gave my chicken, still clucking, to Keith and Ruth and the boys. She survived me, but didn't make it back to Mekomba.

A few days later, another group went on their overnight at the same location. It had rained, leading to a near disaster for them. A runner came into the village shouting that a large tree had fallen over, pinning Karla underneath it. They thought her back might be broken. None of the staff knew the camp location, but since I had been there only a few days before, I led the rescue party to the site. Why they needed me when a runner had just come from the site, I don't recall. Perhaps he needed to give a report to the village president. The staff planned to carry her to the road where a truck should be waiting.

Upon arriving, we saw that the 80-foot-high tree was uprooted and lying on the ground. Termites had weakened the tree and at just the wrong moment for Karla, who had been setting up her camp nearby. The upper, smaller end of the tree pinned her down. Had the larger part of the trunk hit her, it probably would have killed her. She couldn't feel her legs, but ants living in the tree feasted on her and she felt them! Once they removed the tree, we prayed for her as the men carried her to the truck. A makeshift bed was in the back of the pickup, but the ride must have been excruciating over the rough dirt track. They took her to the hospital for X-rays. Afterwards, she remained at the center until the orientation course finished. God answered our prayers. We learned after a year she recovered without surgery and could walk with no after effects. It was an amazing answer to prayer.

Love,

L

————————

Dear Harriet,

After Karla's accident, the U.S. ambassador to Cameroon paid us a visit. He heard a bunch of Americans and others were living in Mekomba and decided to see how we were getting along. How he discovered this information, I don't know.

He arrived in a black sedan with an American flag flying from the front fender. He was dressed in a suit and tie. After he parked at the president's house, we investigated what event we might be missing. He greeted us and we told him why we happened to be living in Mekomba. We told him the people had welcomed us warmly and had taught us many important aspects of living in a rural setting. The president of the village and the chief spoke a few words of welcome. As the ambassador left, the chief slipped him a small handwritten note.

Soon after this unexpected visit, the district chiefs came to call on the president. They demanded to know what the villagers had done to these foreigners, causing their ambassador to visit!!! It took quite a bit of reassurance from our staff to convince them that nothing untoward had happened. The ambassador was just visiting his people. The district leaders took the chief to task for slipping that note to the ambassador. They feared he had asked for money. As expected, a hierarchy existed for such meetings and protocol had broken down. It was an excellent introduction to life in Africa. I should have paid more attention.

Love,

L

—————

Dear Harriet,

In March, as our five weeks in the village ended, the villagers prepared a feast for us. Someone killed a monkey while hunting, so that became the main dish. They served it in a stew so spicy that I still don't know how monkey meat tastes. It was rather stringy, as I recall. They did NOT have *baton d'manioc* (a stick of cassava)!

We reflected on the hospitality and generosity of our African friends, even if we could not communicate well. Our household looked back on nights playing UNO by kerosene light, unable to see the colors of the cards. Standing in a shallow basin, washing with a plastic cup dipped in a bucket of cold water would soon become a distant memory. Trying to dry off and get into our clothes and shoes without getting our feet muddy no longer presented a problem.

In March we returned to the center in Yaoundé where our training had begun, and one of Ken's daughters, the three-year-old, excitedly exclaimed they now had "a white glass potty." Oh! the joys of running water, even if it was cold. We no longer took flush toilets for granted. In the middle of the course, Keith and Ruth's luggage arrived. So, back in civilization, they washed up everything they borrowed and returned it. As I mentioned before, I hadn't even missed the things I'd lent her.

We debriefed for a few days and arranged the next stage of our journey. During training, they changed my assignment from Kenya to Sudan. I knew it did not thrill my father, as Sudan shared a border with Libya, the land of Muammar Qaddafi. Dad thought I was entering dangerous territory. All those factors made him nervous. The job was for three years. Ken, Judy and their three girls, Jill, and I prepared to proceed to Nairobi, Kenya (considered the last major point of civilization before entering the wilds of Sudan). Jill and I would head up to Juba, Sudan. I had completed years of study in linguistics and now the orientation course. I wanted to start work.

But first, we had to get OUT of Cameroon. None of us had forgotten how tricky it was to get IN! We departed for Nairobi on Easter weekend, and flights were overbooked. The staff advised us to arrive three hours early for check-in, so we took care to follow that advice. Jill and I brought our backpacks, while Ken and Judy and two of the children took one small suitcase each. We carried our winter coats, as we couldn't fit them in the luggage. Ken once again handled the check-in procedure, since he showed such a gift for this role. He checked our bags through to Nairobi, though later we discovered that was a mistake. The airline handled overbookings by taking off an hour early. Those who arrived in time traveled, and those who came late didn't. That was one flight we were determined NOT to miss.

We located the exit leading to the tarmac and huddled around it. Ken instructed each of the children what to carry; the smallest one was to run as fast as she could. He lined up his four hand-carry pieces OUTSIDE the exit. We waited like sprinters for the signal to GO! When the agent gave the all clear, a predictable rush for the door began. We were ready for that. Jill shoved one poor unfortunate man out of the way with her backpack while Ken and the family dashed out, grabbed their bags and ran. I followed them, with Jill just behind me. Glancing back, I saw the next man's briefcase caught sideways in the door, which stopped everyone else. We raced on and, not surprisingly, found ourselves the first ones on the plane. We selected our seats, stowed our gear, and smugly waited for the others to arrive.

The uneventful flight from Yaoundé saw us back at the port of entry city of Douala. Once inside the terminal, we settled into the air-conditioned restaurant and ordered Cokes at the actual price. We felt very proud of ourselves as we reminisced about our adventures in Cameroon. There was plenty of time for reminiscing, since our flight didn't leave until the early hours of the morning. At midnight, the restaurant closed, so we collected our hand luggage and headed to the empty check-in area. With no chairs, we sat on steps or stood around. I wandered off to a door to take a peek outside. The weather was balmy, and I thought nothing could spoil it.

Just as I turned to go inside, men approached. I sensed all might not be well, but I had nothing of particular value. As they got close to me, they grabbed my arm and tried to steal my watch! I must have screamed, though I don't remember now. Ken ran over to help me; the men scuttled away. After that, I stayed with the others, and we experienced no more trouble!

Airline staff filtered into the airport to prepare for the Nairobi flight. Who appeared at the booth? Yes, the same "lucky" agent who enabled us to fly Yaoundé three months before stood ready to check us in. He greeted us, handshakes all around. "How did you find your stay in Cameroon?"

"We enjoyed our visit and learned a lot."

"Where are you going now?" he inquired.

"We are flying to Nairobi. Are our names on the passenger list?"

"Oh, it seems they missed you once again. Never mind, here are your boarding passes." The clever man thought, *Get them on this flight before they multiply!*

Then he asked about our luggage. The staff in Yaoundé should have checked our bags only to Douala. The agent in Douala should recheck them to Nairobi. He found our suitcases himself in the baggage claim area, tagged them, and sent them on to the plane. If he had not done that, I guess our baggage might have stayed in Cameroon! Ken's relationship definitely paid off.

With boarding passes in hand and luggage checked, we entered the passenger lounge to await our flight. While enjoying the comfortable, padded seats, I got into an interesting conversation with another English-speaking Cameroonian. We expected an announcement regarding our departure, but never heard one, so we were startled when other passengers left the lounge. We jumped up to follow them. We caught glimpses of those passengers just ahead of us as they turned corner after corner through an endless maze of corridors. We hurried to catch up, but as we turned one corner, we only caught another glimpse as those ahead rounded another. The chase continued until we reached the security check.

Jill, Judy, the children and I made it through with no problem, but they kept poor Ken. Judy and the children waited for him as the guards inspected him thoroughly. Jill and I got onboard and found seats. Anxiously, we waited for the rest of our party, wondering if seats would be available on this very full plane!

Meanwhile, Ken cleared the security check, and they navigated the last series of hallways. On previous journeys, we had gone onto the tarmac to board the plane, so that's what they did. But this time, the passengers boarded via the jetway. There they stood on the tarmac, asking the ground crew how to get aboard. In the end, someone rescued them and, by a miracle, five seats remained. As soon as they buckled in, we took off for Nairobi.

Another colleague traveling to Nairobi was on this flight and recognized us. We became especially grateful to him when no one came to meet us at the Nairobi airport. He hired two taxis and directed them to our accommodations. What a blessing! We arrived with our luggage to begin the next stage of our African experience.

Love,

L

Chapter 3
Transitions

Dear Harriet,

A year before leaving for Kenya, I had the chance to meet several Kenyans who were living in the U.S. They mentioned that most African Americans were from West Africa. I asked how they knew. They told me they could tell by the body shape. I didn't understand, but tucked that bit of information away in my head for later. After arriving at Jomo Kenyatta Airport, I understood what they meant. East Africans look significantly different from West Africans. It's hard to describe, but I remember the thought hitting me forcefully.

We rode through the streets of Nairobi, Kenya in amazement. The city was more developed than Cameroon. Of course, Mekomba wasn't comparable, we had seen little of Yaoundé, and none of Douala. Nairobi was full of skyscrapers and wide four-lane avenues. Flame trees, related to our mimosa, lined many of the streets. The flowers are brilliant red and they bloom just before the rains come. I saw plants I thought of as houseplants that were the size of a house! Poinsettias were eight feet high. There were bottlebrush trees, so called because the flowers look like colorful red bottlebrushes tipped with gold. The colors were startling. Plants grew everywhere, and I took great interest in photo-graphing them because I felt color-deprived. Butterflies and birds provided more awesome color, and I wished to spend my entire day sitting in the garden.

Gorgeous homes boasted inlaid wood floors, clean white walls, large windows, and interesting African paintings and carvings. But finding thick bars on every window, along with huge padlocked gates on every outside door, gave me cause for concern. Wealthier residents had large guard dogs and hired guard services to protect their property. High walls surrounded the compounds, sometimes with broken glass or barbed wire on the top.

Nairobi in the 1980s was much like the American West. There were good and law abiding people, but there was also a criminal element that took advantage of an opportunity. Not infrequently, gangs of robbers entered a house, not only to steal but also to attack the inhabitants with *pangas* (machetes). Security continues to be a big issue. The guesthouse manager advised us to be out of the city center before 6:00 in the evening. Even in a car, it was unsafe for women to drive alone at night. I'd never lived in such a dangerous place.

People travel on the left side of the road. As a pedestrian, it became essential to look carefully in both directions when crossing a street. Kenyans drive fast, resulting in two kinds of pedestrians: "the quick" and "the dead." Roundabouts are an interesting feature introduced by the British. There is a large circle at the intersection of two major streets. The center may include sets of traffic lights, billboards, or decorations. Drivers choose from three sets of lanes going around the circle. To turn left, they should be in the leftmost outside lane. From the center lane, cars go straight across, while the rightmost inside lane is for turning right. When entering the roundabout, drivers look ONLY to the right for a gap in the approaching traffic. Sometimes stop lights halt the oncoming traffic. Otherwise, it is a free-for-all.

I found it humorous that the Swahili for roundabout is *kipilefti* for 'keep left'.

Traffic jams were common. No matter the temperature, have the windows closed. Thieves on foot reach inside, grab whatever they want, and take off through the rows of cars. To catch them requires leaving your car to give chase, but of course, that is impractical, so they get away. These unhappy experiences occur to both expatriates and locals.

Petty theft occurs frequently. I received one good piece of advice: Keep your hand in your pocket so no one else has theirs in it! One colleague carried a large wad of cash into town to buy furniture. Knowing the dangers of being robbed, she put the money into her bra. While walking to the store, she suspected that someone might have his hand in her bag. She reached in and felt a hand that wasn't hers! She grabbed it, held on and shouted, "Harami, harami!" (Thief, thief!) The man became alarmed when he couldn't escape and this woman continued shouting and slapping his hand. He began saying, "Pole mama, pole!" (Sorry mama, sorry!) In the end, she let him go.

Further advice includes:

Carry nothing that is irreplaceable, such as photographs of family.

Don't wear expensive jewelry.

If you don't have to have it, leave it at home.

After a couple of weeks, Jill received her visa for Sudan. She completed her final purchases of a mosquito net, cheese, and salami before flying off to Juba. I remained in Nairobi waiting for my shipment, a half-container of "essentials," which had been sent on a slow boat to the port in Mombasa. To pass the time, I offered to help in the office. SIL wanted to set up an office, including buying land, to develop a center to support its work in East Africa.

I phoned lawyers and real estate agents to help complete the purchase of the new property and did other odd jobs. Years later, someone in the Nairobi office asked me if I was new. I said, "No, but you obviously are!"

In late April, I realized my shipment wouldn't arrive soon, and I should go on to Sudan.

Love,

L

Dear Harriet,

I ended up living in various people's homes while waiting for my shipment. Our small guesthouse couldn't accommodate all the visitors who were coming and going. After ten days, I was "farmed out" to an Austrian family. It was my first experience with Germanic people. I developed a lifelong interest in finding out how those from other cultures and lands live.

One night, they invited a German couple to dinner. There was no work for me in the kitchen, so I listened to the men converse. I was listening to them talk, understanding nothing because they were speaking German and I didn't know the language. After ten to fifteen minutes, they realized I wasn't taking part, so they switched to English. I inquired if they had any difficulty under-standing each other since they came from different countries. "No," they said, "We understand each other without a problem." Then I asked if the same were true for the Swiss. The Austrian expressed his opinion, saying, "Swiss German is not a language, it is a disease of the throat!"

My host told me about his one excursion into southern Sudan. He worked in the cotton business and decided to check the quality of cotton there. He traveled overland to Juba and knew when he had crossed the Sudan border from Kenya as soon as he saw a man wearing nothing but a pair of flip-flops and carrying a bow and arrow. He found Sudanese cotton was not usable for his purposes, so he never returned. I don't know how many years had passed since that trip, but I couldn't get that image out of my mind. What was I getting myself into moving there?

While residing with this family, I dropped my passport at the Sudanese embassy to obtain an entry visa stamped into it. In case you don't know, to enter most countries you must get permission before you arrive at their airport. Also, since I was applying to work, I needed a business visa. Well, after a few days, I went around lunchtime to collect my passport. While sitting in the waiting room, I glanced at pictures in an Arabic-language magazine. I paid no attention to others, but became aware that someone had entered and everyone else stood up.

I remained seated with my magazine, debating whether I should stand up (right answer) or just act ignorant and continue to sit there (wrong answer). I chose the wrong answer. The well-dressed gentleman came over to ask the reason for my presence at the embassy. I smiled and said I was picking up a passport. He returned my smile and departed to the offices. Within moments, someone called me back, and here was the same gentleman sitting behind a desk in a tiny office. He asked me a few questions, which I answered as respectfully as possible because I suspected he was the ambassador. In a few minutes, he left the room and thereafter, one of the staff ushered me to his actual office. And indeed, he was the Sudanese ambassador.

He talked about Sudan and offered to lend me three books to read so that I could familiarize myself with the country where I had applied to live. Then, he invited me to go to lunch with him. This prospect did not thrill me. To buy time, I explained I should ask for my boss's approval. Once I informed my Nairobi-based director, he thought it was a wonderful idea for me to have a meal with the Sudanese ambassador and give him lots of information about our work in the south.

On the appointed day, I walked to the guesthouse to be collected. I waited several hours before he drew up in his chauffeur-driven Mercedes. The ambassador met the Sudan Airways flight at Jomo Kenyatta Airport, which is on the opposite side of town from where I lived. Meanwhile, the Safari Road Rally completed their run through Nairobi, stopping all traffic. When the ambassador's car turned up, restaurants had closed, so he suggested we should have lunch at his house. I felt less certain about this arrangement, but what could I do? I almost failed to recognize him because, instead of the suit and tie he had been wearing at the office, he was dressed in traditional clothes. He had on a white *jallabiya*, often referred to as Arab robes, a white turban, and leopard-skin shoes.

Men wearing typical
Sudanese jallabiyas.

Other male employees from the embassy were at the house when we arrived. I was the only woman visibly present, though I expect others were somewhere preparing food. He offered me a drink, and I chose a Coke. He seemed pleased that I did not take an alcoholic one since the Qur'an forbids drinking alcohol. I assume he had it in the house for visitors. Lunch comprised various roasted meats that were tender and delicious. After the group consumed two or three trays of meat and bread, the male servers brought out a new dish. His Excellency informed me this tray contained a northern Sudanese delicacy, but I was free to refuse it. It looked raw, so I passed. Later, I learned that in northern Sudan they eat raw liver flavored with hot pepper, lemon juice, and bile (yes, like out of a gallbladder!). I was glad to have forgone that opportunity.

Months afterward, while in the meat market in Omdurman buying some lung to feed the cat, I remembered this meal with the ambassador. A customer requested bile. The butcher took a piece of intestine and draped it over his thumb and finger, pressing down to form a small bowl. Into that bowl, he poured a bit of bile from a filthy ceramic jug. He tied off the top, cut it free from the rest of the intestine, and accepted the customer's money. I sent a prayer of thanks, yet again, that I had declined the invitation to try that delicacy.

After the meal and more conversation, they invited me to watch them play poker. They conversed in Arabic, so I didn't understand any of the content. After an hour of "scintillating" activity, I wondered how hard it would be to get home. I glanced at my watch and my host immediately asked if anything was wrong. I explained this was supposed to be a lunch engagement and the family I was staying with were likely concerned as to my where-abouts. He called for his driver, who took me home. It was the most unusual social event I have ever experienced.

My last glimpse of the ambassador was at his office. I returned his books on my way to the airport, ensuring I would NOT have another meal with him. SIL's training hadn't prepared me for dealing with high-level government officials when I did my coursework. That omission was clearly an oversight on their part. So now you know: When everyone else stands up, join them!

Love,

L

———

Dear Harriet,

Having returned the books and holding a visa in my passport, I boarded the Sudan Airways plane to Juba. Juba is approximately 800 miles north of Nairobi. In 1982, it was the largest town in the southern region, population 150,000. I stayed in the SIL compound while they sorted out my paperwork. My accommodations were in a guesthouse, a set of rooms, apartments, or a house run by an organization where their visiting employees and guests stay. The daily rate charged is cheaper than most hotels. I met the team working in Juba and got acquainted with the markets and various transportation options. After a mind-blurring few weeks, the time came to travel north to Khartoum.

Map of Sudan[1]

It is important to speak Arabic, as you noticed when you visited me. When I arrived in Sudan, the first task they gave me was to learn that national language. My boss reckoned correctly that the best place to do that was in the capital, Khartoum (1,000 miles up the White Nile from Juba). Once again, I hopped on the local airline for eight months of Arabic study. Little did I imagine I was about to experience one of the greatest changes in my life.

It hadn't occurred to me to inquire how long the flight would be. I just knew that Beth and Bruce were meeting me. Two hours into the trip, I expected we should have arrived. *How far is Khartoum from Juba?* I wondered. Just then, I felt the plane slow and bank. Clearly, we would soon land. I peered out the window, expecting to find the nation's capital. What did I see? Brown. The Sahara lay below us. *Surely there's a city there somewhere!* I thought. I looked more closely and, sure enough, there was a vast sprawling metropolis spreading over the desert. From that height, it appeared almost completely brown. The streets were brown, the trees were brown, the people were even brown, but not for the same reason. Layers of dust covered the streets, trees, plants, and buildings!

Shortly, we landed at the airport, and I stepped out into 100°F with the wind blowing like a hot blow dryer. I hurried to the terminal looking for shade. The heat had infiltrated there as well, and it felt like I'd walked into an oven. Since it was an internal flight, there were few formalities, and my suitcases came out quickly. I searched for a familiar face, but only saw men wearing white dresses with leopard skin shoes and white turbans on their heads. I tried to read the signs giving instructions but discovered that was impossible, as they were written in Arabic. For the first time in my adult life, I understood what being illiterate meant.

I stood around for some considerable time, or so it seemed. I didn't know where to find my friends, what to do if I didn't find them, or how to ask. Later, I learned many people speak some English, but at the time it didn't look like a very promising prospect. Finally, my friends turned up. Bruce and Beth had chosen to sit outside while waiting for me, enjoying the breeze. They assured me I had arrived on a good day since it was cooler than usual. A dust storm (*haboob*) had hit the night before. While these storms make a mess of your house, they cool things down. I was glad Bruce told me or I would not have recognized that it was cooler. As a friend once said, "I didn't understand how far the range extended!"

We took a taxi to the nearby SIM mission guesthouse. To this day, that place has a special spot in my heart. We walked into the grounds, which had green grass, plants and trees and a lovely spacious verandah. I would have paid extra just for the shade at that point. Inside, electricity powered a fan to create a breeze, and they had ice-cold water to drink. I have since learned never to travel (even across town) without water. Now, forty years later, that cold drink remains a vivid memory. My adventure was truly beginning.

Love,

L

Chapter 4
Language Learning

Dear Harriet,

My assignment in Khartoum was to learn to speak Sudanese Colloquial (spoken) Arabic. I needed to absorb as much of the language as possible, so it was important to start immediately. Let me clarify something about the Arabic language. Originally, the Qur'an was written in Arabic, and Muslims believe these are the very words of Allah. However, the Qur'an was written centuries ago, and no one actually speaks that way anymore. So, scholars have developed what is called literary Arabic, a standard that is used in published material. All persons literate in Arabic need to know literary Arabic, and any literate person in the Arabic-speaking world can read it. However, no one actually speaks literary Arabic. Each country and even regions of a country speak a local dialect which is called colloquial Arabic. This version of Arabic is almost never written and can differ considerably from literary or Qur'anic Arabic. In Sudan, people speak Khartoum Arabic; in the south, people speak a very different version known as Juba Arabic.

However, before my studies could begin, I had to have a place to live. Within twenty-four hours of my arrival, colleagues told me about a house where I could stay with an English nurse who was working at a local clinic. I went along to see it and to meet Gaynor, the woman who had offered to share her home with me.

The house was in Omdurman, an older, more conservative part of the city. It was at the intersection of two major roads, *arbaiin* (40th street) and *arda*. There was a roundabout at this convergence of streets, decorated with a small version of the Eiffel Tower. The compound itself was spacious, surrounded by ten-foot walls. The single-story house had four rooms: a bathroom, bedroom, dining room, and office. You may wonder if there was a kitchen. Well, it was outside on one of the wide verandas. The kitchen comprised a table covered with a plastic cloth, a gas cooker (stove and oven), and a small cupboard. The bathroom door was near the oven, and that bathroom sink served as our water source. That room contained some cabinets for storing food, pots, and pans. The bathroom was where we washed our hands and took a bath. Other functions normally associated with an American bathroom were found in a small room on the opposite corner of the veranda. Our refrigerator was in the dining room. My bedroom was to be in what had been the office.

The Eiffel Tower
Roundabout near
my home.

The kitchen on the Omdurman house
verandah.

So, within forty-eight hours of my arrival in Khartoum, I was installed in my new accommodation in Omdurman to live with Gaynor, my first British housemate.

The house itself was from the colonial era, with mud-brick walls about two feet thick, a zinc roof, and outside access from every room. Thick walls kept out the heat during the day but also absorbed heat. When the outside temperature cooled down in the evening, the walls radiated heat to the inside.

With four outside doors, to lock up the house when we left meant checking that three of the doors were locked from inside. We exited through the bathroom door and hid the key on the verandah.

All the doors had screens except the bathroom door. Since that door stayed open most of the time, we had LOTS of flies in the house. I became very efficient at using a fly swatter and sometimes succeeded in killing several flies in one swat.

Gaynor parked the car and Land Cruiser under a temporary shelter on the east side of the compound. Our house was in the southwest corner. But we were not alone there. Malyet, a Dinka man and former leprosy patient, made his living as guard and carpenter. He lived with his son in a small house in the northwest corner of the compound. During a visit to their home village in the south, they had found Akec (a CATCH), a young relative about nine years old and very sick, whom they brought back to Khartoum for medical treatment. She stayed with us for months and attended school for the first time in her life. She tried to teach me to read Arabic, but was not very successful.

Our house had two air coolers, one in each bedroom. No, these are not air conditioners, but what we would call swamp coolers, similar to what they use in Arizona. An air cooler looks like a large metal box sticking out of a window or wall. The cooler has huge windows on three sides. On the fourth side is a nose about a foot square that fits into a hole in the wall. Water feeds into the bottom of the box and is then pumped to the top by means of a small water pump and a piece of hose. When the water gets to the top, there are three tubes directing the water to each of the windows. The windows have troughs at the top with slits in the bottom so that water from the tubes goes into the troughs. The slits let water filter down onto grass mats filling the windows. Louvered openings hold the mats in place and let air flow through to the mats. The air passing through the wet mats cools by evaporation. The cooled, humidified air blows through the nose of the cooler via a large fan powered by a small motor and a belt. This system drops the temperature about 20° if conditions are not very humid. With so many small parts, keeping them all functioning was a major challenge. The cooler in Gaynor's room stayed broken more than it worked, but mine functioned pretty well.

An air cooler with one of the 'windows' removed. Inside is the large fan.

When there was too much dust, I suffered from headaches while sleeping outdoors. So, I chose to sleep inside with my air cooler on. That worked well until my cooler broke. While we waited to get it repaired, I stayed inside with a bucket of water beside the bed. I dipped part of the sheet in the bucket and put it over me. The fan evaporated the water, cooling me off enough to sleep for an hour or two before waking up in a sweat. Then, I re-dipped my sheet. Evaporation is a wonderful thing!

Khartoum claims the prize for being the hottest capital in the world! Beginning in March, the weather heats up so that in May and June the afternoon temperatures reach 120°F (50°C). The humidity stays in the 50 to 60 percent range. In July, the temperatures drop to only 110°F, but the humidity soars to 70 percent. Rainy season happens in August, and the temperatures vary substantially, but humidity remains about 70 to 90 percent. September and October are hot and similar to July, only more humid. About mid-November, the temperature cools down at night—the sign that winter is coming. Did I mention I arrived in Khartoum in the middle of April? What an introduction!

Have I mentioned we didn't have a washing machine? Yes, for the first time in my life, I hand-washed my clothes, sheets, towels—everything. My skills were mediocre, but at least my clothes were exposed to soap and water. One day, having washed out several things, I took a scarf, dripping wet, to the porch, and hung it up. I returned to the sink and picked up the next items to hang up. By the time I took the twelve steps to the washing line, the scarf was already bone dry. Towels dried in a matter of minutes.

Our house had a telephone, but it only worked once during the seven months that I lived there. Gaynor paid the bill regularly, hoping one day it would be useful. Electricity was another thing. Power cuts were a regular feature for most homes, especially during the hot months. However, our house was on the line with a hospital. The government's policy was to keep the army and hospital electricity on, if at all possible. Fortunately, water suppliers had a similar policy, so we normally had water, even if the pressure was very low. If I had to do without water or electricity, I would much prefer having water.

I soon learned not to open windows during the day to let air in because the heat also comes in! To get maximum benefit, close the windows by 10:00 a.m. and don't open them again until 4:00 p.m. or later. Of course, without screens on the windows, one must close them again by 6:00 p.m. to prevent a mosquito invasion, but that's another story. Most people sleep outside in the cooler yard (or garden, as the British prefer to call it).

On that note, I shall close for the evening.

Love,

L

Dear Harriet,

Gaynor spent several years in the northern part of Sudan working as a nurse before filling in for a Dutch nurse in Omdurman. She spoke wonderful Arabic, and I envied her for that skill. She was friendly with another English family who had been in Sudan for eight years and also spoke fluent Arabic. I remember thinking, *I could never make it here for eight years.* Years later, it was quite a shock to realize I'd been in Sudan for fifteen years.

Gaynor taught me a lot about Sudan and Sudanese culture and also introduced me to a good number of longtime expatriates. (When residing in a country other than your country of origin, you are an expatriate. It took me a while to get used to that word.) She also introduced me to English food. I should note that the English are not renowned for their flavorful meals, but since I got hungry several times a day and had no idea what was available, I gratefully received anything.

Up to this point, I had not had much contact with Sudanese, so it was time to jump into my Arabic study. My colleagues put me in touch with their Arabic teacher, a young man named Daoud (meaning David) (pronounced da OOD); he had taught the language book I planned to use many times, so he was well qualified as a teacher. We met twice a week at my house for two hours each time.

Daoud patiently went over the drills and the pronunciation, correcting my mistakes and praising me when I did well. The rest of my day, I memorized dialogues and verb conjugations, trying to get my mouth into the strange shapes needed to pronounce those guttural sounds. During one of our breaks, he explained that he was an orphan, and thus his marriage prospects were very poor. He was studying law at the university.

After a few months, I engaged a second teacher, Sitt Josephine. She also taught foreigners to speak Arabic, but she did conversational practice. This was an excellent complement to my lessons because I could expand my vocabulary and experience "real conversation."

Leoma with Sitt Josephine during an Arabic lesson

Besides studying for many hours, it was important to get out and visit people. I mentioned Omdurman was a more conservative part of town. That was true politically, socially, and linguistically. Many

Sudanese in this area did not speak any English at all, so when I began to "get out there," Arabic was essential. I made one of my earliest visits with Gaynor. She knew a local family through relatives she had met in the north. During some festival, they invited us to have lunch with them. We entered the women's section and sat in a pleasant sitting room, chatting with the ladies of the house, Amaal and Su'aad. I could catch snippets of the conversation by this time, but occasionally, someone addressed a question directly to me. Sometimes Gaynor translated the question into English, and then I tried to answer it in Arabic. At other times, I could understand the question, but took so long figuring out how to say an answer that the conversation had moved on and the question was forgotten. As we washed our hands before the meal, one woman told her friend (in Arabic), "This is the one who doesn't know any Arabic!" I wish I had known how to say, "Well, I understood that!" Unfortunately, I hadn't learned those words yet, so I just fumed.

One of my fellow Arabic language learners had met Amani, a high school student, and traded off English lessons for Arabic practice. I visited her, too, and found her family very interesting. It was my first opportunity to look at how a Sudanese family lived. Since this girl was in school during the morning, we called on her in the afternoon after lunch, from 4:00-6:00. In the 1980s people came home from work or school around 2:00, rested, unless they were cooking, and ate lunch at 3:00 or 3:30. They served tea after the meal, just in time for visitors. It was unheard of for a visitor to arrive and not receive boiling hot tea in a fruit juice glass!

Visiting took place outside in the *hoosh* (yard). The women brought beds out of the house and placed them in shady parts of the yard, along with small tables (for setting down your tea). Men often sat in chairs with metal frames and woven plastic string for the seat and back. The advantage of a string chair was that air passed through easily. When the temperature is dropping from 110 degrees, any opportunity for a breeze is welcome. Women often sat on the *angareb* (wooden bed). The frame was made of wood. The "mattress" part was, much like my rope bed in the jungle, a mesh of rope or colored plastic string woven in lovely patterns. Usually, a cotton mattress was placed on top. They covered the mattress with a beautiful and skillfully embroidered cotton sheet. There was commonly a matching pillowcase covering a rock-hard cotton pillow. Some of the older women preferred to sit on a woven plastic string mat on the ground. In the not-so-distant past, chairs were uncommon and older women were used to sitting with their legs straight out in front of them. I tried that for about thirty seconds before I gave up. There might be a small, square *banbur* (a low seat or footstool), made in similar fashion to the wooden bed. The most common seat in any Sudanese kitchen was a *banbur*.

Conversation was the most common pastime. Gossip filled much of the visit. It was not unusual for a female to be asked the price of her shoes or how much rent she paid, or where she found some rare commodity. I, of course, presented a whole new avenue of investigation, once I had enough language to understand the questions and form answers!

That was where my Sudanese high school friend became helpful. Amani spoke more English than I could speak Arabic, so she translated for me and helped me enjoy getting acquainted with her family. After they got to know me, they tried to marry me off to various male relatives. Sometimes we watched television, but I never understood what was being said. The people speak colloquial Arabic, but read all books and media communication in literary Arabic. Additionally, the Qur'an is in classical Arabic. These three "Arabics" are listed as different languages in linguistic classifications because they have different word orders, vocabulary, and sound systems. It makes learning the language more challenging.

One of my most memorable visits with Amani was when she took me to visit her school, which was within walking distance of my house. She attended an all girls' school and there were about sixty students in her class. The teacher took my presence in stride, continuing with the lesson as if I were not there. I remember she read out of a textbook, stopping occasionally to explain the meaning of a word. Of course, the book was written in literary Arabic while the girls spoke colloquial Arabic. Thus, they would not necessarily understand or know all the words either. The teacher wrote the new word on the chalkboard. The girls copied down as much of the information as possible in small exercise books. When it came time for exams, they had to memorize everything they could and later recall it verbatim for the test. As I understood almost nothing, well actually nothing at all, I became bored pretty quickly. Apparently, the girls were, too, because they became fascinated with my hair.

As I would learn some years later, Africans do not pay much attention to hair or eye color, since everyone's hair is black and everyone's eyes are brown. Since my hair is light brown and very straight compared to theirs, the girls behind me decided to try to braid it. Well, it braids fine, but in the end it wouldn't stay that way unless they tied it with something. So, as soon as they let the hair go, it unraveled itself, much to their delight. They liked to touch my hair and skin. I think they wanted to see if the "white" rubbed off. I doubt they learned much from their lessons, but we had an enjoyable time together.

My other notable visit was to a Ramadan breakfast. Amani and her family invited Beth and me to break their fast one evening. Ramadan began six weeks after I arrived, in June, when it is blistering hot by anyone's standard. During Ramadan, Muslims should fast from food and drink from about 4:30 a.m. until around 6:00 p.m. When the weather is brutally hot, it is a very trying time indeed.

On the appointed day, I went to Beth's house so we could go together to Amani's. However, since most things start later than the invitation says, we did not rush and were still visiting at Beth's house when Amani came to get us. "They could not start eating until we arrived!" she informed us. So, we grabbed our things and followed her to her house. It was then that we learned any other meal may start late, but not a Ramadan breakfast. As soon as the call to prayer comes, it is a sign that the faithful can drink, pray, and eat. From then on, I've never been late for a Ramadan meal!

Upon arrival, we discovered a large mat on the ground covered with a vast array of foods, many of which I had never seen in the market. The people import specialty items as part of celebrating Ramadan. We had figs floating in sugar syrup, several kinds of beans, apricot leather, the usual stews, salads, and fruit. It was indeed a feast. We joined the family on the ground, reaching into the different pots and bowls, using only the right hand as is customary, and enjoying the delicious food.

The women had cooked and slept much of the day; so, after breakfast, they headed out to visit with friends. The market and shops remained open most of the night. Around midnight, everyone ate "lunch" from the food left over from "breakfast." After sleeping for a few hours, they got up about 3:30 a.m. to eat "supper." Porridge or cornflakes with milk were popular. They tried to catch a few more minutes of sleep before the call to prayer came, announcing the beginning of another day of fasting. By the end of Ramadan, people shifted their lives around so they were awake at night and asleep during the day. For those who went to work, the worst part of the month of fasting was sleep deprivation.

Love,

L

Dear Harriet,

During my orientation course, I had learned how important greetings were. A colleague in Ghana was at a service station when another car pulled in. The foreign woman driver stopped, jumped out of the car and asked the station attendant for directions to a place nearby. He gave her instructions that seemed totally wrong to my colleague, who was watching this event unfold. After the woman left, my colleague said, "I thought that building was in the other direction!" "It is," came the reply, "but she didn't greet me." That story has stayed with me, and reminds me to begin any conversation by saying "Hello!"

So, the first thing in my language learning was to master a greeting. As I watched how people greeted one another, I realized how true the story I've just related to you presumably was. Sudanese spend a long time greeting each other. If they are just being introduced, the greeting is short, but if they know each other, it goes on forever. They say, *"Salaam aleekum, Allah yisallimak, Allah yibarak fiik,"* which is all to say, "Peace be with you, may God give you peace, and may God bless you." They both repeat this over and over while shaking hands with their right hands, then putting the right hand on the left shoulder of the other person and giving a brief hug. Then they go back to shaking hands, and hugging again, sometimes with even a kiss or two on the cheek. It made one feel as if the person was glad to see you. After they get past this part, they ask about the other's family and mutual friends. Once assured that everyone is fine, they begin a conversation or go on their way, depending on the situation. It appeared as if everyone remembered each person they had ever met!

Another very useful word that I learned very early on was *itfaddal*. *Itfaddal* does not have an equivalent in English, but essentially offers permission for the person to do whatever they want to do. If you knock on the door, *itfaddal* means you can come in. If you are standing up, *itfaddal* means you can sit down. If you are not eating, *itfaddal* means you can eat and if you've been eating, it means you are free to stop.

I'm not going to give you a whole Arabic course, but there are a few words that you must know, and now is a good time to explain them. If you learn no other Arabic words, you need to know the "IBM" of Sudan. The IBM is: *Insha'allah,* "God willing"; *Bukru,* "tomorrow"; and *Ma'alesh,* "sorry, too bad."

On one occasion, I squeezed into a *taraha* (shared taxi) with several men. During the half-hour ride over the White Nile Bridge and into Khartoum, one of the men struck up a conversation with me in English. When we arrived at our destination, we got out. But my "new friend" asked to meet me back there later that afternoon. I realized he was trying to pick me up, and I wondered what on earth I could say to extricate myself from this plight. In answer to a silent prayer, the words *insha'allah* came out of my mouth. It worked beautifully, and honor was spared on all sides. It is a great replacement for "maybe."

Marian had worked in Sudan for many years, living in the country's southeast among the Nuer people. She told me that once a week she traveled from her tiny village to the nearby town to shop.

There was a particular item that she needed, but each week when she asked for it she was told *insha'allah, bukra,* "God willing, tomorrow." Now *bukra* (BOOK rah) is similar to the Spanish *mañana*, which has little if anything to do with the day after today. After a few weeks, Marian returned to town yet again. As soon as they saw her, workmen on the roof of the shop called out, "Come, come, today is *bukra!*" The item had at last arrived.

Now, we come to *ma'alesh* (ma LESH). It has many meanings, too, depending on your intonation and the event. I've seen parents comforting tiny, irritated children who were hot and uncomfortable with "*ma'alesh.*" When I asked for something that wasn't available, whether it was food, postage stamps, or a seat on the airplane, people said "*ma'alesh.*" If there was an accident, someone tripped and fell on the sidewalk or had a flat tire, you would hear a chorus of people saying "*ma'alesh.*" I explained this word to a Finnish colleague, and she asked how you knew which of the meanings were intended. I demonstrated various pitches of the voice, which ranged from mild indifference to deep concern. "Oh, that word would never do in Finland!" she exclaimed. "We use so little intonation the meaning could only be, 'Oh, too bad!'"

Your last phrase for today is *al hamdu li'llah,* "God be praised." When electricity has been off for twelve hours, the temperature is over 100°F and power finally returns, you say "*al hamdu li'llah*" (el HAM du lee lah). When at last you get to the front of the queue and they have something you want, you say "*al hamdu li'llah.*" After a dust storm comes while you are away from home and you return to find that you had closed all the windows, you gratefully say "*al hamdu li'llah.*" So much of life is outside our control. In the West, we think we have control, but we don't. It is a figment of our imagination. Living in Sudan taught me that, while I'm less able to control my life, I can rejoice when things go well, be patient when things don't, and at the end of the day say, "*al hamdu li'llah.*"

Love,

L

———————

Dear Harriet,

You may have wondered how I got money during those months of living in Khartoum. I received my salary in U.S. dollars in the States, but those dollars had to be turned into usable currency, namely Sudanese pounds. Now, in most countries you and I have visited, it is easy to carry enough money with you for the few days or weeks that you are going to stay. Mind, in 1982 there were no ATMs. You exchanged your cash in the bank or at a money exchange. Well, things were more comp-licated when you lived somewhere else. It was even more challenging when that somewhere was Sudan.

One of my first errands involved going to a local bank. The administration had instructed me to take a dollar check to open an account. This request seemed easy and standard. I opened the account, and then the clerk explained I must wait to take money out of the bank until the check had cleared through the U.S. bank. The process would take about six weeks. It sounded like a long time, but I had sufficient funds to last me.

I returned six weeks later, and they assured me that I could withdraw my money. By this time, I knew the exchange rate, which was $1.00 to £s0.90 (Sudanese pounds). When I asked for my money in Sudanese pounds, the clerk looked shocked. "No," he said. "Take your money in dollars and go to the local exchange as you will get a better rate."

Well, I'm not opposed to getting the best deal I can, so my friends took me and my money to the local exchange. There the rate proved to be better, $1.00 to £s1.250 (1 pound and 25 piasters). So, in the bank, the Sudanese pound was worth more than the dollar. At the exchange, the dollar was worth more than the Sudanese pound. Interesting. As we walked to the exchange, several shady-looking individuals sidled up to us and asked if we wanted to change our money. My friends cautioned me not to trade money with them as they might give a better rate, but it was illegal.

I came to understand there were two markets: a legal black market (white market) sanctioned by the government and an illegal black market that was not. The legal black market exchange was available only in Khartoum. So, if an organization had a significant amount of money to exchange, it was worth flying to Khartoum and changing it at the official exchange offices. Are you now totally confused? Join the club.

Love,

L

Dear Harriet,

Gaynor traveled to England for a vacation just as Ramadan began. I was only a few weeks into my Arabic study and no one else on the compound spoke English. It was an unnerving time, as Gaynor left me with instructions to stock up on supplies, especially sugar, during Ramadan. During this month, the government gave a double ration of sugar. But after Ramadan, there would be serious shortages of most commodities because so many of them were used up during this month of fasting. In order to get bread, we sent someone to the bakery at 5:00 a.m. So, at the end of May, with my limited language skills, I took charge of our little household.

Finding oil, milk, flour, sugar, and any imported item proved challenging. Once I found locally available items, they were not expensive, but because of price controls on everything, the supply was also limited. If they grew it in Sudan, then it was available, so long as it didn't have to be processed. For example, they use tomato paste in a lot of Sudanese cooking. But getting tomato paste was often challenging because the factory that processed the tomatoes closed for six months of the year when tomatoes were not available. Thus, the supply of tomato paste soon dried up.

You may wonder what I ate. For breakfast, I enjoyed homemade granola and yogurt. Cereal was $3.00 a box (which was expensive in 1982), so I made granola out of Quaker Oats, which came in a sealed tin can, peanuts, and sesame seeds. The sesame included lots of dirt, so it took a good bit of cleaning. For the yogurt, I made up powdered milk and put a starter in it. I left it in the bathroom overnight and even nighttime temperatures were warm enough to set it. If I forgot to put it in the refrigerator in the morning, it became VERY strong.

Lunch, served about 3:00, was our hot meal of the day. Vegetables like carrots, eggplant, tomatoes, cucumbers, potatoes, and zucchini were available most of the year. But from December through March, green beans, peas, cabbage, and lettuce were in season. The shops carried a few canned goods such as peas or pineapple, but they were expensive. Butter cost $4.00 per pound. Margarine was available from Nairobi via the Juba commissary for $2.50 for 2 pounds. Beef and lamb were plentiful, but I didn't know how to cook lamb. Pork was rarely available, as Sudan is a Muslim country and Muslims may not eat pork. Some Christians raised pigs, so occasionally we could find pork if we knew the right sources.

For supper, Gaynor and I ate an egg with cheese, bread and maybe peanut butter and jam.

I've always been fond of fruit, and Khartoum has an interesting variety of dates, grapefruit, bananas, guavas, oranges, and mangos. The cheese was not what we expected at home. Feta, a crumbly, salty cheese, was common. Delivery men brought it to the shops in large tins filled with brine. The shopkeeper weighed it in quarter- and half-kilogram amounts and put the cheese in thin plastic bags. When I got it home, I often rinsed it with water to get the salt out. After a hot, dry day at the market, it was just what I needed to replace the sodium my body had lost.

After a few hours in the scorching sun, upon returning home, I started drinking water. Notice I said "started drinking," because I couldn't stop after gulping the first glass. After the second glass, I might pause and sip the third one. Then the sweat would break out. It took from sixteen to twenty-four ounces of water, at least, to restore enough fluid to my body that I could actually sweat again. What a country.

One day, while walking to the bus stop and marveling at how hot it was, I felt a cool sensation on my arm as it brushed past my skirt. I became aware of the evaporation process being caught against my skirt, creating a momentary coolness.

The greatest shortage during that time was fuel. Our household had two vehicles: a Land Rover that ran on diesel, for Gaynor's medical work, and a compact car that ran on gasoline. Gaynor's Sudanese driver looked after the Land Rover, so we didn't have to worry about it. The car was another matter. They rationed fuel to three gallons every other day. People lined up by 6:00 p.m. to be among the first when the stations opened at 6:00 a.m. We had a station around the corner from our house. As the queue lengthened, cars blocked our driveway practically every evening. Someone had to sleep in the car all night to prevent it from being stolen. If you employed a driver or a guard, you assigned that job to him. If you didn't, you got to sleep in the car yourself.

After sleeping in a car all night, few people felt like working. As this situation continued for weeks, and weeks turned into months, less and less work was getting done in offices. The government finally took action, announcing that petrol stations could not open until noon daily and no one was allowed to queue before 11:00 a.m. Any car in a queue had the license plate removed, and the owner had to pay a fine to get it back.

Our friend John owned a large car and his wife, Deborah, drove their children from Omdurman into Khartoum to school every day. They needed fuel regularly, so they hoped this new regulation would be an improvement. At 11:00 a.m., John drove over to queue up, but found he was 100th in line. By the time he reached the station, the pumps were dry. The following day, he watched to see what was happening before 11:00. Sure enough, around the corner, cars were parked at right angles, facing in the opposite direction from the station, any direction except in the station's. At 11:00, they turned around and formed a quick queue! The next day, John did the same, and got fuel. This regulation didn't last very long because even fewer people went to work. People coped with the many frustrations and inconveniences by telling jokes. The many shortages were fertile territory. One joke I heard goes like this:

A man queued up for several days to get a bottle of cooking gas. Having obtained that, he queued for sugar, then for gasoline, and again for bread. This pattern continued until he came to the end of his patience. He was determined to kill President Nimeiri for causing all these shortages. When he arrived at the palace where the president worked, the guard asked him to state the nature of his business. He said, "I have come to kill Nimeiri." "Oh," said the guard, "just stand in that queue over there."

Another joke told of a man who went fishing and caught a Nile perch. But when he got home, he found he had no knife to clean it, no charcoal to heat it, and no oil to cook it in. So, he returned the fish to the river and threw it in. As the fish swam away, the man heard the fish call out, "Long live Nimeiri."

By the time Gaynor returned in June from her vacation, Ramadan was over, we had plenty of sugar, and my Arabic had improved considerably.

Love,

L

———

Dear Harriet,

While we were unable to get many things in Khartoum, one thing we did have was nice powdered milk. I'd never used powdered milk and was dubious at first. Using fresh milk took significant effort to process to make it safe to drink. With fresh milk, I had to sieve it through cheesecloth to get out the dirt and cow hairs and then boil it to prevent tuberculosis and other dreaded diseases. After that amount of work, powdered milk looked and tasted pretty good. We bought brands imported from the Netherlands that came in 1-lb. or 5-lb. tins. The tins were worth keeping as well! All things considered, powdered milk wasn't that expensive. One cup of milk powder dissolved in one cup of tap water, followed by one of boiling water and a tablespoon of yogurt starter, was just perfect to make a tub of fresh yogurt every few days.

Some well-meaning people or businesses in Europe decided they wanted to help the poor Sudanese Christians. So, asking no one, they shipped two tons of milk powder to the Episcopal Church in Sudan. I lived kitty-cornered to their headquarters and visited with the officials now and again. They were shocked and then horrified to learn of this gift of milk. The donors sent no money to pay for customs or the storage charges that increased daily. No resources had been made available to transport the milk to Khartoum and, once it arrived, where would they put it? How would they distribute it? The office staff comprised two men, one bicycle, and a dog.

In the end, they sold the milk powder in Port Sudan and used the proceeds to pay off the customs and storage. They brought a few bags to Khartoum to give to church families living in the compounds adjoining ours. We got a little, and I have to say, it was dreadful. First, it couldn't be mixed with water, not even using a blender! I've never worked so hard at something so unproductive. Once it was sort of mixed, it tasted revolting. None of the church families wanted to use it, as the milk powder we bought in the market was of much higher quality. So, I fear much of the donated milk got tossed out.

Such deeds of charity went awry all too frequently. One German firm shipped a huge power-generating system to Khartoum to ease the frequent power cuts. This system was in one large piece and came with its own special truck to haul it to Khartoum. After it arrived in Port Sudan and was loaded onto the special truck, they soon arrived at a large bridge. Was the bridge strong enough to carry such a heavy load? The engineers checked it out and, sure enough, it wasn't. If that were the only vehicle on the bridge, the weight would be too much. From the report in the *Sudanow* magazine article on this boondoggle, I learned they couldn't take the power station apart or the sand would ruin the internal workings. As they couldn't get it across the bridge, they abandoned the generator in the desert. My uncle suggested they set it up on the Port Sudan side of the river and run a long wire to Khartoum. I think they should have returned it to Port Sudan for use there. Instead, it became one of the many "white elephants" left by the wayside in Africa.

Love,

L

———————

Dear Harriet,

During the summer, Hillene (pronounced as hill-LANE), one of my colleagues from Juba, came up for a visit. It must have been in August. Her brother and sister-in-law were in Khartoum to see her and they stayed for a week in the Hilton hotel (nice digs, if you can afford it!). But when her brother and his wife left, she came to stay with me.

One of her favorite activities was to go to the American Club pool to swim. Our house was thirty to forty-five minutes and at least two bus journeys to the pool. So, I usually went swimming on Sunday afternoons, but dedicated the rest of my week to activities in my part of town.

By the time Hillene visited, I had stopped noticing how much dust there was. It's interesting how quickly we adapt to our environment. Hillene pointed out that when she asked for an air form to write a letter, I dusted it off as I handed it to her. If she asked for a stamp, I dusted it off before I gave it to her. In fact, I realized that when writing a letter of even one page, I kept dusting off the page to keep the pen from clogging up. The fine Sahara sand blew into everything, even sealed plastic bags in closed drawers.

Hillene decided to return to Juba and get to work. She flew up on Sudan Airways, but rumors suggested it might not be flying to Juba. We traveled downtown to the office to see about booking her on a flight.

We arrived early at the airline's office, where we met Marian. She had returned from a vacation in Ethiopia and wanted to get to her village in eastern Sudan. On her way to Ethiopia, Marian had tried to fly the 500 miles to Khartoum from Malakal, but the planes had already stopped service there. Instead, she had ridden up on the Nile steamer. She figured correctly that the plane would not be flying to Malakal. She opted to trade in her Malakal ticket for one to Juba. Then, one of the mission planes that flew all over the south of Sudan would fly her to her village. Marian was older and more experienced in the ways of Sudan, so we suggested she go first to show us what to do. Inside the Sudan Airways office, she walked up to the counter and explained her situation to the agent. He agreed to sell her a ticket to Juba. She had to go to another part of the office, pay the extra amount (since it was a longer trip), and come to collect her ticket. She headed off to the cashier.

It all looked too easy! I approached the agent, remembered to greet him, then explained that my friend also needed to travel to Juba. His reply was, "I can't sell you a ticket."

"Why can't you sell me a ticket?" I asked, smiling and trying to be as friendly as possible.

"The plane isn't going to fly," came the reply.

"Why did you sell the other lady a ticket if the plane isn't going to fly?" was my reasoned response.

With great patience, he said, "She had a ticket. If you have a ticket, you can buy a ticket. Do you have a ticket?"

With increasing amazement and confusion, I said, "No! I don't have a ticket! But why sell the lady a ticket if the plane isn't going to fly?"

"Because she has a ticket," he replied. He had concluded that I was thick in the head. And I guess I still am.

I persisted until he sold us a ticket but, as predicted, the plane did not fly. Marian ended up taking the steamer back to Malakal, from which a mission plane took her to her village. Hillene flew, at great expense, on a USAID flight.

I learned later from friends living in Malakal during this time that their mail reached them only once during the five months without plane flights. On that occasion, the mail came on the steamer. The postal workers were reprimanded for sending it that way since the envelope was clearly marked AIR MAIL. My friends reported that the mistake did not happen again.

Not long afterward, I learned my shipment had arrived in Juba. The heat of Khartoum was taking its toll, so I decided to take a brief break in Juba and return to the airline office to inquire about flights. "Are there flights to Juba?" I asked. (I was learning the correct way to get the information I wanted.)

"Yes, there are flights every day to Juba," the staff member proudly announced. I started to tell him when I wanted to book my flight. But he interrupted, saying, "But they have canceled all flights until after the Hajj" (the yearly pilgrimage to Mecca in Saudi Arabia).

This time, I knew not to argue. I was learning that in Sudan things happen "every day, but not some" days. In the end, I got to Juba on the USAID plane.

We flew in a small twenty-seater jet. I had never been on a plane where a passenger could sit and chat with the pilot during a flight. It intrigued me to see the many dials and instruments, so I asked the pilot what those instruments did.

"Oh, not much," came the reply.

"Why ever not?" I asked.

"There is nothing on the ground for them to read!" came the surprising answer. He explained that when you flew in southern Sudan, you were flying by the seat of your pants. You followed the Nile as long as possible, then veered away from it to find your destination. Then you came right back, or you could become lost in the vast expanse.

He pointed into the distance and asked if I saw some hills. I stared hard and could just make out a small bump on the horizon. "Well, fifteen miles south of those hills is Juba," he said. I commented it seemed hazy, but the pilot assured me it was clear that day. When the locals burned grass in the dry season, then it was truly difficult to see.

After a couple of weeks in Juba, I felt sufficiently refreshed to return to Khartoum and learn more Arabic.

Love,

L

Dear Harriet,

Having returned from Juba, I needed to get in touch with Daoud, my Arabic teacher. He lived in Bahri, also known as North Khartoum. I didn't know where, but Bruce and Beth had a P.O. box for him. They had written him and he received their letter in a few days. So, I sent a note to say I wanted to resume my lessons. I posted it at our local post office and then waited. After nearly three weeks, Daoud turned up. I asked why it had taken so long, and he explained he just received the letter!

I mentioned this long delay to Bruce and Beth. They asked how I had mailed it. I said I put a regular stamp on it. "That's the problem!" they exclaimed. "We sent ours airmail!"

"But he just lives across the river! Why on earth does it need an airmail stamp?" I still have no answer to that question, but evidently it takes extra postage to cross a bridge.

Dick and Saundra were also studying Arabic in Khartoum for a few months. Before coming, Dick mailed some books to Khartoum from the U.S. Among them was a book about Islam and Christianity. Dick repeatedly inquired about his books, but no one at the post office admitted knowing anything about them. They moved to Juba, but Dick came up to Khartoum for something. He stopped by the post office once more to inquire about his missing books. This time, the clerk said, "Wait." He hunted around and pulled out a mailbag. Inside were Dick's books, all except the Christian ones. The shipping box was gone. When the supervisor asked what the clerk was doing, he replied, "These are his." Clearly, someone did not approve of Christian literature coming through the mail. So, they confiscated them.

Love,

L

Dear Harriet,

One day, I wandered into a local shop at the end of my street and met Layla, the owner, who seemed to know about everyone in the neighborhood. She had lived in England for a few years and spoke excellent English. Layla was beautiful! I loved to watch her expressive face and listen to her clear, crisp Arabic as she dealt with various customers who came in. She appeared quite savvy with salespeople and held her own with the men. So, I visited her several times a week. Besides, she had frozen popsicles in her freezer, my favorite being guava flavored.

Layla's father had married her off when she was very young to a doctor who worked in England. After the wedding, she took her first plane journey. He liked to smoke, so he sat in the smoking section. She was alone in the non-smoking section. Since she spoke little or no English, she didn't even know how to select a meal or fill out the arrival form the flight attendant gave her. Their relationship ran smoothly for a time, but she missed her family. Then her husband started to beat her. She must have sent word to her family because they allowed her to return home and her husband divorced her. She remarried, but things didn't work out with husband number two either. So, she lived with her brother, or he was living with her; I wasn't entirely sure. By the time I met her, she had started this little business to support herself, her brother, and maybe some other family members. I believe she had two children, a boy and a girl, both by the second husband.

After several months, she invited me to a wedding—not hers, but a relative's. Sudanese invite everyone they know to these occasions, so she thought to include me. It was quite an event! She tried to get me to wear my normal clothes to her house and then change, but I just put on my good clothes. She had an old car, and it spluttered across the White Nile Bridge into Mogran (pronounced MOO gran). Years later, I would move to Mogran (the confluence of the Blue and White Niles), but at that time, I did not know where I was. She lived in a simple house with beds in every room except the bathroom. There was an indoor bathroom, but no toilet paper. I'll explain about that later.

After our light lunch, she told me to rest, as we would be out late. I lay down, but soon her brother came in and lay down on another bed nearby. I felt uneasy about that and only snoozed. The room's one small window had a crack through which smoky incense entered. The smoke triggered an allergic reaction that, before I finished my afternoon rest, started into one of my dreadful sinus infections. Being sick did rather spoil the remainder of the evening for me.

But let me return to that crack in the window. The window was very near the area where the women do their *dukhaan* (smoking). There is a small hole, about four to five inches wide, in the women's section of the courtyard. They put burning charcoal into the hole, then sandalwood incense on top of the coals. The woman strips off her clothes and sits over the hole so that the smell of the incense seeps into her skin. In order to stay "decent" and hold in the scent, she drapes a woven grass mat over her with space in the middle for her head to stick out. It takes an hour or more to get the full effect. But once that incense gets into the pores, the scent stays for days.

Preparations for having a *dukhaan* treatment.

As darkness descended, I found the bathroom. It was the sit-down variety, but without a seat. That is not an uncommon occurrence, but it makes sitting more challenging. Also, there was no toilet paper. The common way to clean oneself is to use water from a small jug. Then one uses the left hand for whatever else needs doing. Needless to say, you never bring your left hand to the table or wave with it or serve with it, and this is the reason.

Well, we put on our "glad rags" and headed off to the wedding. Layla was gorgeous in a silver lamé *tobe*, and I felt very much like the poor relation. This part of the wedding involved the bride wearing a long white dress and the groom a black suit. There was a band and everyone danced. There must have been a thousand people at the football (soccer) stadium. We sat at small metal tables in chairs designed for a torture chamber. These straight chairs had a metal frame. Plastic string was woven across the seat and some on the back for "support." The bottom was all right, but the back was sheer torture. The metal bar hit me across my shoulders long before my back ever got to the string part. The pain inflicted by the bar caused me to slump in my chair, trying to fit into it. When my back hurt in that position, I straightened up, and the bar bored into my shoulder blades again. I learned to lean forward a lot.

Layla had many friends to catch up with at this wedding. At one point, she was listening intently to a friend telling a long and involved story. Periodically, Layla made a clicking sound, rather like we would use to get a horse to move. After listening to this sound several times, I interrupted the story and asked her what the click meant. She looked puzzled and then laughed. No one had asked her that question before. "It means, 'go ahead, I'm listening,'" she replied. The story continued, as did the clicking.

Each person received a bottled soft drink and a plate of food, all of which I could easily eat using one hand. There was a boiled egg, bread, salty cheese, a piece of tomato, and *basta* (sweet pastry rather like baklava). They say *"basta"* because there is no "p" sound in Arabic. After everyone had eaten, the dancing started. The band inspired me to get up to dance. Layla explained that the traditional Sudanese dance involved a woman moving only her head and neck in a sensuous way while the man strutted about her and snapped his fingers over her head to show his approval of her performance. The youth preferred disco music, which replaced the traditional music after a little while. In later days, when the Islamic government banned men and women from being together on these occasions, it made me sad, as it discouraged a nice tradition.

Around 11:00 p.m., we loaded onto buses and traveled to the outskirts of Omdurman for the last part of the wedding ceremony, where the bride puts on a sexy red dress and performs the "dove dance" for her husband. As much as I wanted to attend, my sinus infection had caught up with me, and I was feeling pretty horrible. As they passed my house, I asked to get off and went home to bed. I was grateful to Layla for her kindness and her gracious friendship in inviting me. It would be a decade before I had another opportunity. Years later, when I returned, the store had changed hands, and she had disappeared into the millions of Khartoum inhabitants.

———————

Dear Harriet,

Khartoum, Omdurman, and Bahri (North Khartoum) are huge cities of about a million people each. The Niles separate the three "towns." The Blue Nile comes into Khartoum from the east, having originated in the highlands of Ethiopia. It separates Khartoum from Bahri. The White Nile originates in Uganda In the south and flows north through the swamps of southern Sudan at a leisurely pace until it reaches the capital, separating Khartoum to the east from Omdurman to the west.

At Mogran they join and form "the" Nile, which flows north to Egypt. "The" Nile separates Omdurman from North Khartoum. In places, the Nile is at least a half mile wide. So, greater Khartoum is a BIG city, and traveling from one part to another without a car was challenging, especially in the extreme temperatures. I preferred to stay in Omdurman during my language-learning phase.

Sometimes I took buses when I went to another part of the city, most of them about ready for a museum. Their windows didn't close and often the doors didn't either, possibly because they were so full. Passengers hung out the doors while the buses were moving. During difficult times, people just grabbed hold of a bus window ledge from the outside, lifted their feet off the ground, and rode along. When the bus stopped for a light or because of traffic, the hangers-on would let go to rest their arms and hands until the bus started again. Then they reached up and grabbed the window ledge until the next stop. I don't think they had to pay the fare.

Boarding a bus became my first problem. I had to get a bus that had passengers but wasn't full. The philosophy was that a bus could not leave the station unless it was full. With fuel in short supply, buses rapidly had a full load of passengers traveling to or from work. However, during those peak times, for those traveling against the flow, it proved difficult to get enough passengers at the station to fill the bus. They could pick up passengers along the route, except that the unwritten rule required the bus to start full.

This practice had two unfortunate effects. First, it could take ages to leave the station. Second, if the station was too far away, but not far enough that passengers wanted to disembark, there was no space for you, so the bus wouldn't stop.

Once you got a bus to stop, the next problem involved getting on. Men and women entered through different doors, women in front, men in back. I tried the front door, but found the women quite aggressive, so I used the back. The men behaved less forcefully, at least with me. I normally ended up standing all the way to my destination as the seats filled up quickly and I seldom got one. I never learned to be that insistent.

The bus would jerk to a stop or lurch forward to start. However, standing proved easy since with so many people around me, I couldn't fall over. I remember standing in a super-crowded bus and it occurred to me I was the only white person there. I realized what it meant to be a minority and learned a valuable lesson. In Sudan, I felt no fear or discomfort at being surrounded by people with a different skin color. These folks were welcoming and helpful and I felt at ease, even surrounded by strangers.

Once we were moving, the conductor would come along to collect the fare. Conductors tended to be slim young boys, a decided advantage when weaving in and out through tiny spaces and among many people. They snapped their fingers to announce their presence and kept track of who had paid and who had not. When passengers paid, they got a little slip of paper as a receipt. The fare was only a few pennies. Sometimes people would pay for themselves and me, even though they had never laid eyes on me before. I learned to have money in my hand when I boarded the bus, as I often couldn't get to my bag in the crowd. Pickpockets rode buses in those days but were not as great a problem as they are now. Today you need to keep your hand firmly on your bag or it may disappear, along with your money.

The last problem involved getting off. As I saw my stop approaching, I tried to have a coin in hand so I could use it to bang on the nearest metal object. If a coin was not available, I snapped my fingers and everyone shouted at the driver to stop. When I stood far inside the bus, it often proved challenging to reach the door and disembark before the driver started off again. I remember standing in the crowded bus in the heat and humidity, sensing sweat trickling down the back of my legs. I wondered if there were any telltale signs as I disembarked.

On one of my last trips into Khartoum before returning to Juba, a bus stopped for me. Men already crowded the rear door opening, so I placed the ball of my right foot onto the step and reached in among the white robes of other passengers to grasp the handrail on the side of the door. I waited for someone to get off. No one did, and the bus moved. I lifted my left foot and off we went, this time with me hanging out the rear door and my sisal basket swinging in the breeze. I found a small spot for my foot and held onto the ledge above the door with my left hand. The breeze felt heavenly, and I enjoyed letting it blow through my hair. Then I heard a voice saying in English, "You got on there like a seasoned traveler!" I looked back and saw Syd, one of my language-learning colleagues, tucked up on the back window ledge with his son Benjamin on his shoulders. I laughed and asked where his wife was. She was standing inside, only a few feet away from me.

The other male passengers became upset, as it was unacceptable to have a foreign woman swinging around outside the bus! I had to come in. "Where?" I asked. They shuffled about and by the next stop, they had squashed me inside.

Riding the bus offered an adventure, but it was not always comfortable, so my public transportation of choice was a "box," a small Toyota pickup with a roof over the back and two long benches down each side of the truck bed. Boxes carried twelve passengers in back and two in the cab with the driver. The money collector sat in a seat or hung off the back. Unlike in Kenya, where there is "always room for one more," fourteen really was the limit. The boxes followed set routes, and a color code showed where they were going. Most of them came into the center of the town, so the stripe of color on the outside clued you in on where it would return. Another advantage of boxes, besides being less crowded, was the freedom to talk with people. It was public enough that I wasn't likely to get "picked up." People were friendly, and it provided a good place to practice my Arabic.

My other form of transportation was the taxi. There were private taxis and shared taxis. *Taraha* (shared taxis) traveled along a set route and the fare was lower than if I had hired a taxi myself. However, when I had done a lot of shopping or was in a hurry or just too tired to deal with life anymore, a private taxi was a good option. I learned from hard experience that as a single woman, I needed to sit in the back seat. Sitting in the front signaled the driver could take liberties. Most drivers were bored, so having a foreigner who spoke Arabic was a pleasant change for them. I got quite a lot of language practice during those fifteen- to twenty-minute trips (which would have taken up to forty-five minutes on the bus). So, on the whole, even though it was more expensive, I got my money's worth.

Love,

L

——————

Dear Harriet,

Gaynor was friends with a Swiss medical team. They regularly held a clinic in a nearby area called AbuRof (Rof's father). Occasionally, Gaynor and I were invited for lunch with them. We started from our house about 1:30 in the afternoon for the thirty-minute walk to their place. The thought *Only mad dogs and Englishmen go out in the noonday sun* invariably came to me. Well, if Gaynor was the Englishman, what did that make me?

My monocultural world was expanding yet again as I got to know these hardworking Swiss folks. George, his wife, Maja, and Rosemary, the Swiss team, started their days about 6:00 a.m. handing out numbers to the sick people already lined up at their door. Various Sudanese doctors took turns seeing patients, but the lab work and organization were up to the Swiss ladies. They saw hundreds of patients every day except Friday and Sunday.

On one visit, they took us on a tour of their laboratory. It was very basic and none of their equipment depended on electricity. It was amazing to see what they could do with so little. Malaria was the most common ailment, but there were others who came with open wounds, expectant mothers, sick children. The clientele were mostly very poor people, many of whom I expect would have died if this free service were not available.

By 2:00 in the afternoon, they closed after a very full 8-hour day. That was about the time we arrived, so I never saw any patients. They had simple, healthy meals, and I learned a lot from listening to their stories. George told me one story about how bees can cure malaria. I was sure I had misheard, but no, I heard correctly. The "doctor" picks up a bee and places the stinger on the patient. This is repeated eight times each week for four weeks. Assuming the patient isn't allergic to bee stings, s/he is often cured. This 2002 article says the venom from the bee inhibits the malaria parasite[1].

We usually departed at about 4:30 or so. There was a large thermometer hanging in the shade and I remember it read 45°C at 4:00 in the afternoon. In case you are wondering, that is 113°F! We walked home, and that thought about mad dogs and Englishmen came to me once more.

Love,

L

————

Dear Harriet,

In Khartoum, I learned a great deal about Sudanese hospitality. I grew up in the southern part of the U.S. that is known for its friendliness; I thought I knew how to show hospitality. But after a

[1] https://allafrica.com/stories/199709170 029.html

few weeks in Sudan, I realized we didn't have a clue. The Sudanese welcome total strangers into their homes and ply them with water, sweetened fruit drinks, tea, cookies, and other food. On top of that, they make it seem that you are doing them a favor to share it with them.

Early one morning in late October, a friend and I were out shopping. We met a Sudanese lady and chatted with her about nothing in particular. Before we realized it, she had invited us home for breakfast. She was very insistent and, since we needed to practice our Arabic, we went. She took us to the nicest room in the house and seated us near a low table. Soon a woman brought in a round tray about two feet in diameter loaded with chicken, meat stew, tomato and cucumber salad, bread, *kisra*, fried eggs, and fruit. It was enough food for at least ten people, and there were only three of us. Perhaps there were others who would finish what we left. After breakfast, we enjoyed a glass of water and a cup of sticky, sweet tea.

My first journey outside of Khartoum proved that hospitality extended beyond the capital. That trip took place in early November, when Gaynor invited me to accompany her to Karima in the north, along the Nile. Gaynor had worked in that area and wanted to visit some friends for a week. She decided we should go by bus, as riding on top of a lorry might be asking a bit much for my first journey into the Sahara.

We prepared by buying bread and fruit to take along. For meals, we had boiled eggs and cheese. We took a large container of clean water despite there being a goatskin filled with water hanging on the side of the bus. We didn't know how clean that water was and did not want to risk becoming ill on a trip with few "comfort stations." I noticed that after drinking the cup of water, passengers tossed the last bit of water onto the goatskin. This action kept the skin wet, and the evaporation cooled the water inside. Our "clean" water in a plastic container was tepid.

The scheduled departure was 8:00 a.m., and we expected to reach Karima, our destination, in sixteen hours. The distance was only 100 miles, but over a desert track. We reached the station and found an old bright-blue Bedford truck, converted into a bus. The seats reminded me of school buses at home in Chattanooga, Tennessee. The crucial difference was that, besides the two and one-half seats on one side and one and one-half seats on the other, they folded another seat up in the aisle. Once the passengers were seated in the regular seats, they unfolded the aisle seat so another passenger could sit there. Passengers were not child-size, but adults, so the role of the aisle fold-down seat passenger was to hold everyone else in their seats. The strategy worked well.

Every long journey requires luggage. I took one basket inside with me, like on a plane. There were no overhead bins, so it sat at my feet. Men tossed the rest of the luggage onto the roof and strapped it down. The bus roughly doubled in height with the luggage in place, and I feared it was top-heavy.

The bus loaded for the trip to Karima

Gaynor had booked our seats in the first forward-facing row. The very front row faced backwards toward the rear. This configuration allowed us to get acquainted with the travelers seated opposite us. Gaynor told me it was important to be in the front. She had heard of passengers in the back getting concussions after their bus leaped over a large bump and their heads cracked against the ceiling! (I forgot this piece of advice when I chose my seat for my second journey. I won't make that mistake again!)

One of the younger women sitting opposite us was traveling to a wedding in Karima. Having made some initial attempts at conversation, we discovered that if she spoke English and I spoke Arabic, we got on well. The problem with communicating with a native speaker is that she can choose words you haven't learned. However, when speaking the other's language, we could choose words we knew and the other person understood all of them. Being able to understand what someone else says in an actual conversation is a lot harder than it is in a class!

Boarding the bus was a challenge. The first step was a small ladder that hung perpendicular from the doorway. The bottom rung was two feet off the ground. I was young and agile in those days so I easily made it up. But the lady who turned out to be the one sharing our two and one-half seats was large. She had quite a job hoisting herself up (with a bit of gentle pushing from people behind).

By the time everyone was ready to go, it was about 10:00 a.m. There was one police check about a half hour out, and then we were on our own. For the next two hours, we traveled along as best we could, considering we repeatedly got stuck in soft sand. Whenever the driver was unsuccessful at driving us out, we would see some aluminum skids come sliding off the roof onto the sand. Next, a leg or two would appear in the window, which had no glass in it, and then disappear as men jumped to the ground. They placed the metal skids under the wheels to free the bus from the soft sand. Once we were on hard ground again, they would grab the skids and toss them onto the roof, and scramble back up on top. Off we went to the next patch of sand, and the entire process repeated.

About noon, we got stuck, only this was more serious. The rear axle broke, and we did not have a spare. We got out while the driver assessed the situation. We ate lunch and rested. As we got off the bus, the bottom step (that had been over two feet above the ground) was now level with the sand. The track for the bus was that deep! I remember lying down in the track and realizing that I was invisible to anyone a few feet away since the track was deeper than my body.

While waiting for an axle, we found thorn bushes to sit under for shade. We ate some of our food, drank water, and eventually found sufficient cover to serve as a "comfort stop." As the afternoon progressed and the sun set, the women migrated back toward the bus. We had become a very chatty group by this time; small trials of this sort often bring strangers together.

I decided to sit on the bus, out of the sand near the door. An elderly man across from me was chewing tobacco. As we tried to talk, he spit his tobacco juice out the door and very near my feet. I desperately tried to think of the verb for "spit" so I could ask him not to spit on me. But I'm not sure I would have used it if I had remembered it.

When it grew dark, they decided the women should sleep on the bus, and the men should sleep outside. I found an empty row of seats and stretched out to rest. One man, who seemed to have some mental issues, stayed on the bus. He kept lighting matches and looking around, muttering, *"Dabiib, dabiib,"* which I later found out means "snake, snake." As far as I know, there were no snakes on the bus.

Late in the evening, the driver borrowed an axle from a lorry on its way to Khartoum. The crew replaced the broken one, but it took several hours to do that. At 2:00 a.m. we returned to our seats with our aisle passenger fitted in to hold us in place, and off we progressed through the desert. How the driver identified where to go, I have no idea. There was no GPS available! We did not get stuck in the sand as often at night. During this trip I learned another lesson: Night in the Sahara gets COLD!

One old man tried to keep his feet warm by putting them in our basket of food. No telling what state that bread was in by the time we ate it! I envied others who had brought something (even a towel) to wrap around their heads to ward off the chilly night air. The towel also blocked out the light that blazed from a bare bulb above my head.

Since this was supposedly a day trip, I had worn only a light cotton dress and had taken no sweater or even a scarf. We pulled a blanket out of our food bag and wrapped up in it. The three passengers facing us wanted to share it, and that was fine except for one problem. The man by the window pulled his corner of the blanket over his head, which meant that the cold air blew in under the blanket. I nearly froze to death.

At one point, I was so cold I put my head under the blanket to see if that would help. I was between a *habbooba* (grandmother) and Gaynor, who had somehow fallen asleep. I envied her unconscious state. She leaned over my way, and my head got stuck under the blanket. I struggled to free myself so I could sit up again.

At 6:00 a.m., we arrived at the journey's first "comfort station." They sold tea there, but that was the extent of the "comfort."

There was scarcely even a bush to hide behind for other needs. People washed and said their prayers and then drank tea. It was a wild and wonderful spot, with miles and miles of sand and stark rocky hills in the distance. I do not know where it was, but I was glad the hospitality station was there, and that the driver found it in the dark!

Teashop in the desert on the way to Karima

After that brief respite, we drove on and soon came to various villages where passengers began to disembark. One of the larger villages had a small *suuq* (market), where we stopped for a breakfast of lentils. Gaynor suggested we eat something cooked with nothing raw (such as tomatoes) as that could introduce giardia or other unwanted "passengers" into our systems. The locals asked what had happened to us and why we hadn't arrived the day before. I was glad they had at least noticed we were missing.

A few hours later, we arrived at the wrong side of the Nile. We disembarked while the driver backed the bus down a steep bank onto a ferry. It is important to get out of your transportation during ferry crossings, as sometimes the ferry overturns. You don't want to be inside if that happens.

We reached our destination after twenty-eight hours of traveling. But Gaynor was not sure where her friends lived. She had arranged for us to stay with two Scottish "sisters" (the British term for nurses) who lived in Karima. The bus dropped us off at the hospital where they worked, and one of the other nurses took us to our friends' house. Gratefully, we collapsed and recovered from our adventures.

Love,

L

———

Dear Harriet,

Karima is a typical northern village of one-story mud-brick houses with flat roofs. An eight-foot-high wall surrounded each home to ensure privacy. Each part of the house was separate, with covered walkways in between. The layout was as I've shown below.

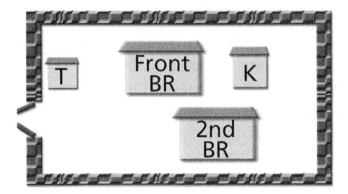

The opening to the left of the sketch is the door to the street. The two larger rooms are bedrooms. In a family household, the front room (Front BR) served as the parents' bedroom and the other room (2nd BR) for the children. As the family grew, verandas were enclosed as bedrooms or a living room. But in this household, the two bedrooms were the only ones enclosed. (I suspect they doubled up during our visit, but normally each had her own room). To the left (T) of the main door was the outhouse and shower. Without an abundance of water, long-drops served better than flush toilets. The small room at the back (K) was the kitchen. Most rooms were under one roof except the outhouse and the kitchen.

In most Sudanese households, men hosted male visitors on the front veranda nearest the main entrance. Women entertained female visitors on the back veranda nearest the kitchen. Some homes have two entrances, one for women and one for men. It is acceptable to move between the two if you are a guest or well-known to the family. At least I've been able to. Single white women have a special status, with privileges a married woman might not have.

The *zeer* is in the windiest location and accessible to all. A *zeer* is an unglazed, oblong clay pot containing water. They fill it each morning. The clay absorbs the water so that it is wet and drippy. There is often a bucket underneath the cone to catch water that drips down. The wind evaporates the water on the *zeer*'s surface, cooling it as well as the water inside, resulting in water that is much more refreshing. The cooling costs almost nothing and does not depend on the erratic electricity. They tied a cup to the *zeer* so anyone could help themselves to a drink. The Sudanese seem comfortable all using the same cup, a custom that I found a bit worrisome.

Zeers provide cool drinking water.

Long-drops vary, as they did in the Cameroonian village. Most have no seat, just a hole in the concrete slab. Women have to perch over the hole in a squatting position and aim carefully. As long as you have good knees, it works. On the other hand, if diarrhea hits, it is not a pleasant experience. These latrines can be twenty feet deep and I always approach them with some care, as I have a fear of heights. I couldn't see down through the little hole, but if the slab gave way.… Well, best not to think too much about that. They frequently take showers in an adjoining room, with the water ending up in the same large pit.

The kitchen is a separate room to prevent fires from spreading to the rest of the house. The separation kept smoke and other unpleasant things like soot from getting on everything. Charcoal burners provide the most common cooking source, but more well-to-do homes also had a cooker with a gas bottle.

With no closets in rooms, people use wardrobes instead. I'd not seen one of these before going to Africa, but soon became accustomed to the more limited space they afforded. We slept on simple *angarebs* with a three-to-five-inch-thick cotton mattress. We used the beds inside during the day and then carried them outside in the evening. Sleeping outdoors under the stars provided a magnificent view, and there were no electric lights to spoil it. It was also much cooler outside, and a blanket was very welcome.

Love,

L

———————

Dear Harriet,

The advantage of sleeping outside overnight was waking up with the sun. The disadvantage was that soon after sunrise, the flies attacked. We were far enough from the Nile that we didn't need to use a mosquito net, which left me in a very vulnerable position in the morning. I came to hate flies. Once the sun was up, the heat intensified, and I didn't want to be covered up with a sheet or anything else. So, I promptly moved the bed inside to be in the shade!

The Sudanese, of course, are used to the climate. When they sleep, whether at night or during the day, they cover up completely with a sheet: head, feet—everything. It keeps off the insects, but when I tried that, I thought I might die from the heat. Whenever the Sudanese go anywhere else in the world, they're cold!

The next event was morning tea. Breakfast normally takes place mid-morning, so an early cup of milky tea and cookies (or biscuits as the British call them) took the edge off my appetite. Our hostesses left for work by 7:00 a.m. Gaynor and I took our time getting ready for the day. There was more time for reading, writing letters, and just sitting around in Karima. Mid-morning, we went off visiting.

No, we didn't know anyone in Karima other than our hosts, but that was irrelevant. I walked along the street and noticed that the gates to the compounds were open. The open gate was a signal to clap my hands or knock on the door, and then step into the compound. The lady of the house greeted me like a long-lost relative, even though she had never seen me before. Hospitality, as I have mentioned, has the highest value in Sudan and it is their joy and privilege to make you feel welcome and part of the family. Even with the few words of Arabic I used, they praised me for my fluency. I knew their compliments were far from the truth, but I enjoyed hearing it.

One afternoon, I returned alone to where we were staying and sat in a chair on the veranda for a quiet time to read. After a half hour, a neighbor came by to bring something and discovered I was there by myself. Yikes! What a dreadful state I must be in to be alone. "Aren't you afraid?" she asked.

"No," I replied, "I like it that way."

She left, but in a few minutes, she sent her son, a boy of twelve, over to stay with me and keep me company. We ran out of conversation topics within fifteen minutes, but that didn't matter. Sudanese don't mind sitting and doing nothing so long as they are keeping you company. So, he sat there, and I read until the rest of the household came home. At that point, he left. Being alone is about the worst thing that can happen to a Sudanese person. I learned much later that one of the most severe forms of punishment is to isolate a person from society.

On another day I visited a girls' school and sat in on the classes. The girls thought it was great. I don't know what the teachers made of it. After that, everyone knew I had been there and asked me about it. It is hard to do anything unobserved.

Another day, we visited the hospital where our hostesses worked. They trained local nurses to be more proactive in attending to patients' needs, both physically and emotionally. The hospital provided basic care and was clean and spacious. Those patients requiring very serious attention had to be sent to Khartoum.

The four of us—Gaynor, the two sisters, and I—went visiting together in the afternoons, often visiting other hospital nurses. There was plenty of gossip describing who had married whom, then divorced and remarried, and how it happened. I didn't catch all the conversation, as my Arabic was still less than fluent. But hearing Arabic so much has a positive impact, and I learned more vocabulary. We enjoyed a lot of tea. I noticed a smoky smell that resembled pipe smoke and was told they used goat's milk in the tea, giving it this smell.

On Friday, since no one in the house had to work, we hiked to Karima's most interesting place, Jabal Barkal. *Jabal* means "hill" and this one had enormous boulders that made it easier to climb to the top. The view was stunning, as we could see for miles. The homes appeared to be miniature playhouses. As it neared sunset, we hurried down the other side. The slope was covered in sand so deep we could literally walk straight down. We ended up on the opposite side of the town and had to walk around the hill. The soft sand made walking much harder.

Walking along a Karima road by the date palms for another visit

Gaynor walking straight down the sand on Jabal Barkal

The following afternoon, we investigated ruins near Jabal Barkal. The pyramids are small, and thieves had looted them many years ago. Even so, I learned Sudan has more pyramids than Egypt! I found the most interesting section was at the base of the *jabal*. There is a cave where ancient statues of gods still stand. Centuries ago, priests of the temple dressed and fed the gods as part of their ritual to keep the world running on its proper course. At this time, archaeologists had excavated only a small part of the site. In later years, they discovered much more that revealed new information regarding the beliefs of the ancient peoples and their view of the world. But that must wait for another day.

Love,

L

———

Dear Harriet,

All good things must come to an end, and soon our visit was over. Gaynor planned to go on to Debba, where she used to work. She wanted to say goodbye to friends and then return to Khartoum by whatever means she could. We put her on the steamer, the boat that navigates along the Nile. The next day, I boarded the train on my own for Khartoum. Just before leaving, I visited the local market and bought a dozen pink grapefruit for 15 cents and a dozen white grapefruit for 20 cents. Armed with the world's best grapefruit, several packages of dates, food for the journey, my plastic container of clean water and a cup, I boarded the car. They labeled it First Class *Mumtaz* (Excellent). I had a sleeping compartment I was to share with an older lady, another *habbouba,* like the one sharing our seat on the bus. The young woman who had traveled on the bus with us was staying next door with her uncle. I was glad that there was someone I knew traveling with me. Her uncle had studied to be a veterinarian in England and spoke excellent English. My gratitude for this acquaintance increased later in the trip.

Each compartment had two beds, one up and one down. The *habbouba* had already claimed the lower bunk, so I took the upper one. All my grapefruit were in a large sisal basket with my cup. These items stayed on the floor while I placed my backpack on the top bunk. I settled in and chatted for a few minutes with my new roommate. There were no sheets, but, having learned my lesson from the bus, I used a *kanga* from Kenya, one of those multi-purpose cloths, for my sheet. This time, I did not pack it in my suitcase. I also brought a blanket. For food, I took dates, boiled eggs, bread, and *tahnia*, a block of sweet sesame-seed paste, a little drier than peanut butter. I loved to eat it spread on bread. It has a nutty flavor.

The train set off after I got settled, speeding along at about thirty miles per hour. This narrow-gauge railroad crosses one of the most hostile deserts in the world. There was a restaurant car but, as I found out when the vet invited me to join him, it served nothing but tea. He and I shared a table with three men. They liked the fact that I knew some Arabic, limited though it was. But when they became a little too friendly, I decided it was time to return to my compartment. The *habbouba* asked where I had been, then asked why I hadn't brought her any tea. Culturally, Sudanese women can't go into the dining car, even for tea. The conductor, whose work is to bring whatever the passenger requests, wouldn't bring her any. So, her only option was to grab a quick cup through the window when we pulled into a station. I noticed that during the day, platforms at the various stations were full of vendors offering everything from tea to cotton material, from sweets to fruit. There was little time to check the quality, just make your choice, pay your money and take the item. About that time, the train moved on.

At some point, I lost my cup. This was disastrous! It must have rolled out the door while I was making up my bed, because I never saw it again. Without my cup, I could still drink from my gallon water container, but it was rather heavy. My *habbouba* shared hers with me. She also shared her food with me, and so I contributed from what I had.

I checked out the bathroom facilities in the light of day. On the closer end of our car there was a sit-down type toilet. At the bottom of the basin was a hole through which I watched the railroad ties flash by. At the far end was the "footprint" type, the nearest thing to a long-drop available. I tried the closer one when it got dark, before climbing up to my top bunk. The lights in the hallway worked, but not in the bathroom. I opened the door, took a step inside, then slid in several more steps. Immediately, I had second thoughts, turned around, slid back out, and headed to the other facility. It was cleaner, and the lights worked.

On my return, I noticed it was hard to see. I was wearing glasses since the dust level made using contact lenses impossible. After taking off my glasses, I discovered a thick layer of dust on the lenses. I cleaned them and put them back on, but still couldn't see. So, I removed them again to find the problem. There was yet another thick coating of dust on them. The windows were wide open, allowing as much airflow as possible, and with the wind came the dust. The only solution was to go to bed.

I stretched out on my bunk, only to realize there was no guardrail to prevent me from falling out of bed! I moved to the back side of the bunk and hoped for the best. Through the night we rocked along, the motion gently rocking me to sleep. About the time I drifted off, the train jerked to a stop. I had to brace against the mattress to keep from being thrown to the floor.

Every few kilometers, there was a station where a family worked keeping the sand off the tracks. This family depended on passing trains for food, water, and anything else they needed because there was nothing anywhere near them except desert and sand. This work assignment was known as a "hardship post," and it certainly earned that name. After the personnel dropped off essentials and I had almost fallen asleep again, the engine would start with another jerk. I held on all night to prevent ending up on top of my grapefruit. Most Sudanese women would share the bottom bunk rather than risk the top one. Now I understand why. I got little sleep that night.

Karima and Jebel Barkal are north of the Nile just above
where the map says Upper Nubia

By morning, we had reached Atbara, a town of significant size. We stayed there for several hours while they unhooked the engine from the train. The nurses warned me not to get off, no matter how long we were there. Many people got on in Atbara and if you left your seat, you might lose it. Then you would stand up for the

2 https://www.pinterest.com/pin/572027590146725121/

rest of the trip to Khartoum, and it was still a long way. I took advantage of being still to get an hour of sleep. After that, I washed a bit, dusted myself off and felt very pleased with myself!

That feeling soon changed. An hour before departing for Khartoum, the conductor came by, talking animatedly. My *habbouba* collected her things while the vet explained they were about to take our carriage off the train. They needed it to return to Karima that night. We had to move to another car! I gathered up all my stuff and followed everyone else to the second-class sleeping car. There were three bunks on each wall, totaling six beds in the compartment. The beds were so close together that it was impossible to sit up straight. We all waited until the conductor came by again, then the vet gave him a piece of his mind: We had paid for first class and we had to be put in first class or the railway would have to refund our money.

After some shuffling of people, the *habbouba*, the vet's niece and I ended up in the seated first-class section, along with four other women and several children. There were six red upholstered seats with headrests. The vet sat a few compartments down with some men. Before long, I came to appreciate having the sexes separated. The vet invited me to come and join him, as our chamber was crowded. I sat with him until the men began suggesting marriage proposals. At that point, I returned to sit with the women and encouraged his niece to sit with him. I figured (correctly) that he would protect her, while he had no obligation to look after me. While I was with the men, someone bought a bunch of bananas at one station we passed. He gave me a banana to eat, but when I bit into it, it crunched. I'd never tried to eat a green banana. They are quite bitter. So, making my excuses, I left and tossed it out the window for the local goats to eat.

The women enjoyed that I, a foreigner, could speak Arabic. They all wanted to ask me questions. I cooperated, but eventually closed my eyes and said I wanted to sleep. After an almost sleepless night and the weariness that comes with thinking in a still unfamiliar language, exhaustion won. I didn't actually sleep, but at least I didn't have to interact with anyone. When it was time for breakfast, the ladies got out their food: pigeon, bread, eggs. I got out my stuff, and we all ate together. At the end of the meal, they pulled out the *tahnia*. I looked forward to that until they poured a jar of guava jam over the *tahnia* and then ate it. The flavors and sugar combined were more than I could tolerate. It would be years before I could eat either *tahnia* or guava jam.

In the breezeway behind us, there was a *zeer*. Since we were so close, people often asked for a cup so they could get a drink. The *habbouba* always lent them hers, and I became less and less happy with using her cup! The water in the *zeer* ran low and when they dipped anything out, it was almost pure mud. I offered to let them drink my water, since it was at least clean. But that was unacceptable because it wasn't cold. At least I didn't feel guilty about drinking it since no one wanted my clean but warm water.

After twenty-nine hours, we arrived at the station in Khartoum. I had almost ceased to believe we would ever arrive, so it came as a shock when we did. Finding my way back to the second-class sleeping car where we had left our luggage, I tossed my bags out the window of the train. Then I poured out my remaining water to lighten the load, climbed down the steps, collected my things, and headed for the nearest taxi stand.

After walking everywhere for over a week, I had forgotten about the fuel shortage. With difficulty, I got a shared taxi to Omdurman.

Love,

L

Dear Harriet,

Before leaving for my adventure to the north, I had moved to a new house. Gaynor was substituting for a Dutch nurse. When she returned, Gaynor was handing the work back to her. There wasn't room in our dwelling for three people. So, I moved in with Alison, a Canadian. She lived in the same compound as my English friends John, Deborah, and their three daughters. Alison's house wasn't all that big, but she agreed to share it with me for the remaining two months before I finished my Arabic study and transferred to the south.

After coming back from Karima, I carefully studied the landmarks just to find my new home. Alison was away when I arrived, so I unpacked my things. Deborah suggested I take a bath at their house, using the hot-water heater. Oh, what a blessing hot water was to my tired and dusty body. I felt half the desert was in my hair and covering me, hiding in my nose and my ears. Once clean, I enjoyed a cup of tea, cooked some food, ate, and crashed into bed for a long sleep. Later, we all appreciated the grapefruit, as well as a lot of excellent dates.

The routine here was different. We still ate our main meal midday after everyone got in from work about 2:00 p.m., rested, and then went visiting or continued working in the late afternoon. About 5:30, the children ate their "tea" of bread and jam and cake, before going to bed. The adults also enjoyed tea and biscuits. We returned to our various tasks until about 9:00, when we met for a light supper and caught up on the day's activities.

The middle daughter, Helen, had a pet rabbit. He was allowed out of his cage for a time at night. He was huge, and he loved date pits. He would sit on his haunches and beg for dates. One evening, Alison's cat, Cod, also rather large, made the mistake of joining us. The rabbit sat up and hissed at the cat. The cat bristled and rushed out. I had never heard a rabbit make any sound, let alone one that would frighten a cat!

One Friday afternoon, we were just finishing our meal when John looked out the open door and saw a *haboob* coming. He got his camera to photograph it. We watched in horror as the huge cloud of dust, about 300 feet of it, moved ever closer.

One moment, the garden was green; the next, it was yellow from the approaching dust. We urged John to come inside and close the door to keep dust from filling the house. Just as it reached us, he took one last photo and came inside. Those pictures are worth a thousand words!

A dust storm (*haboob*) approaching

It is funny how quickly I adapted to my surroundings. Dust was part of the environment. So, if I could view nearby buildings, it would be a clear day. If I couldn't, it would be dusty. The sky was always brown or yellow. One day, I exclaimed in surprise, "The sky is blue!"

Alison glanced up and said, "So it is! But you can't go home saying things like that!" After my eight months in this desert city, brown became the normal color for the sky.

Another change you may notice is that my vocabulary has become more British, with the addition of words like "lorry" and "tea" (meaning a meal). As a linguist, it is an occupational hazard.

Love,

L

Dear Harriet,

When I returned from my trip to Karima, my Arabic had improved even more! I could talk about many new topics. All those hours on the bus and the train made a difference. I felt renewed confidence that I was not a failure at language learning after all. I enjoyed visiting and trying to tell stories in Arabic about my trip. My Sudanese friends found my efforts entertaining. We enjoyed some good laughs together.

During one of my last visits with Amani and her family, I explained I would be moving to the south of Sudan to work with a language group there. I did not expect the response I got from this news. They were quite horrified! Amani's mother asked me—in Arabic, of course—why I was going to live with those "animals"!

Shocked at the use of that word, I managed to ask, "Do you know any southerners?"

"No," she replied.

"Well, they are very nice people!" Within the coming months, I would learn how widespread this view was among the northern Sudanese.

After my ten-day visit in the north in November, Thanksgiving was upon us. To celebrate, I headed for the pool at the American Club one hot day. The nights were cooler, but the days seemed as hot as ever. Changing into my swimsuit, I headed to the deep end of the pool and dove in. Yikes! The water felt as though there were ice cubes floating in it. The humidity had dropped along with the nighttime temperatures. The resulting evaporation caused a significant drop in its temperature. I got to the shallow end without drowning from the shock. I climbed the ladder and didn't swim in that pool again for a long time.

The American Club pool

Christmas almost got lost that year. In Sudan, there were no external signs of this major holiday. As an Islamic country, at least in the northern part, there is no motivation to celebrate a Christian holiday. Since I was living with Brits and a Canadian, everything was different anyway. We attended church in the morning, then returned home to open gifts and ate an enjoyable meal together. I wanted to phone home, but none of our phones made an international connection. The time difference was also a factor. Sudan is seven hours ahead of Tennessee, so to reach my parents in the daytime meant I had to call in the late afternoon or evening. I would have an hour-long journey to an international phone, wait for the call, and make the hour-long return journey. I couldn't face it, so I didn't phone home.

The day after Christmas, however, I stayed overnight at a guesthouse which had an international line. It took more than an hour to get through to the U.S., but I spent the night at the guesthouse and didn't have the hassle of trying to get home again.

In the 1980s, to place an international call, it was necessary to go through the local operator. I decided I would try to conduct that discussion in Arabic as my own final examination. The operator thought this was great fun. I explained I wanted to phone the U.S. He took the number and said it would be about an hour before he connected the call. He instructed me to wait near the phone. I waited, and in a few minutes, he called me back. No, my call hadn't gone through, but he wanted to chat. We must have talked for an hour, all in Arabic. It is much harder to speak to someone in a foreign language if you can't see that person. It's amazing how many cues you get from gestures and facial expressions. Those cues are not available when you talk on the telephone.

Finally, after sufficiently entertaining him, or maybe his boss came by, he connected me and it was great to hear my dad on the other end of the line. It was joyous talking with them in person, but they were rather unhappy that I hadn't phoned ON Christmas Day.

Within two weeks, 1982 drew to a close, and I was on a plane to Juba to begin my second year in Africa.

Love,

L

Chapter 5
Reaching Shilluk-land

Dear Harriet,

On January 2, 1983, I arrived in Juba for the third time. This time, Sudan Airways did fly and none of my luggage went astray. I was finally beginning the work that I had spent years training to do.

Khartoum's weather was cool and dry when I left, but upon arriving in Juba, I found it hot and muggy. The neem trees were in bloom. Everyone was coming down with "colds," which I suspected were allergic reactions to the significant amounts of pollen floating in the air and lying in thick yellow sheets on the ground. We held our biennial conference, and I met my colleagues who came in from many parts of southern Sudan. We were an interesting multinational bunch.

On January 8, I received my birthday present. You will recall my birthday is in October. Mom and Dad mailed this gift in August to give it plenty of time to arrive. Have I mentioned that mail to Sudan was slow? Anyway, it came as a nice surprise, and I appreciated it all the more because it was late.

Before leaving the U.S., I had inquired about what I should bring to Africa. The answer was, "Whatever makes you feel at home." Never having lived outside the U.S., I didn't know what items meant "home" to me. Once I got to Africa, I discovered them, but they were not available. So, parcels became important, as they provided a few of those reminders of home, like chocolate chips and autumn leaves.

Letters to Juba proved to be even slower than to Khartoum. First, they arrived in Nairobi, Kenya, and sat there until someone brought them to Juba. Fortunately, we were not the only organization using this method of delivery, so any personnel traveling to Juba collected all the mail for everyone and brought it. Our group often received several mailbags when the mail finally arrived.

One other new experience during these introductory days was a motorcycle lesson. Syd, the pilot, took on the challenging job of teaching me to ride a motorcycle. Now you know I've never been wonderful at coordinating my body and convincing it to do new things like water skiing. Well, skiing must be related to driving a motorbike, because I couldn't get my mind around that either. My feet believe they should control the speed and the clutch, not my hands! Hands are for steering, not speeding up and slowing down. Just imagine the entertainment I provided going up and down the dusty drive, avoiding the neem trees and the people who stood around at their own risk, laughing. In the end, I drove into the guesthouse porch and the motorbike and I hit the ground. I decided then and there that was not my vehicle of choice. I've never ridden another except as a passenger. And, in the words of Forrest Gump, "That's all I'm going to say about that!"

There was the inevitable paperwork to sort out, which meant I had a few weeks in the regional capital, Juba, before heading north to Malakal to work with the Shilluks. Someone suggested that I type *Occasional Papers in the Study of Sudanese Languages, Volume 3*, a collection of linguistic papers. These days, that wouldn't be such a difficult task, but in 1983, no one had thought about having a computer! This was to be the last book of the series typed on an electric typewriter. There were many special characters, so I had to change the typeface ball every few words. In addition, there was an interlinear text to be lined up manually. Interlinear text means that the language being studied is on the first line. A word-for-word translation of the text into English is on the second line and possibly the third line. Here is an example from my favorite text by Eileen. I've included a free translation in the "fourth" line, so you will know what it means. In the original, that was mercifully on a separate page.

kiyi	mí dri	nga	-zo	go'da ni -'a	ání -ka fi	-li lĩmvu
crocodile you		leave			go imperf.	your of enter infin. water
		event-line marker			(croc.)	

Crocodile left and went to enter the water and stayed to eat fish.

ala ri	-'a ĩ'bĩ ání -ka nya -le	i'di.
to stay imperf. fish your of eat infin. this-is-it		
(croc.)		

I particularly enjoyed the *dri* ... *-zo* combinations. Don't you wish you had that job? Remember, it was done on a typewriter. Any mistake of typing or spacing either had to be whited out or the whole page retyped. It's a wonder Eileen and I are still friends. The book had 173 pages. It kept me busy and ensured that I would read it.

I also found time to work in the academic library housed on a screened-in porch. The shelves were open in the front but closed in the back. As such, they kept out a little of the dust that blew around constantly. The books had been cataloged and shelved in a rather strange order, so I decided to rearrange them into an order I could understand, since I was cleaning the shelves. Stacks of books and articles arrived after the previous "librarian" either left or gave up the job. A variety of bugs were living in them and eating them. When I left, everything was on a shelf and available for use.

My final language-learning work project was to describe how Arabic verbs work. Daoud, my Arabic teacher, had worked hard to teach me the different and interesting things that change the meaning of a verb in that language. Take the verb *daras*, "he studied." If the middle consonant is doubled to *darras*, the meaning becomes "he taught." The extra consonant signals a causative, so if someone causes someone else to study, he teaches them. With the verb *kassar*, "to break in pieces," adding a prefix forms a passive *inkassar*, "to become broken." I won't bore you with the whole lesson, but you get the idea. This understanding increased my ability to express what I wanted to say, so I started writing it all down. By the time I got to Juba, it seemed only sensible to finish it. When I got it done, I showed it to three of the Arabic experts in our group. They said I had reinvented the wheel, but it was round. In other words, scholars have defined these rules already, but having analyzed it, I got it right. That was encouraging, even if I wasn't the first to discover it.

Love,

L

Dear Harriet,

In early February, the director and I began making the rounds of officials in the regional government. When the seventeen-year civil war had ended in 1972, the peace agreement allowed the southern part of Sudan (about 250,000 square miles) to be semiautonomous. Three states made up the Southern Region: Equatoria, Bahr el-Ghazal (the Gazelle River), and Upper Nile.

Juba was the capital of Equatoria as well as the Southern Region, and Malakal was the capital of Upper Nile. So far, I've never been to Wau (pronounced Wow), the capital of Bahr el-Ghazal. Each state sent representatives to Juba. The regional minister of education had responsibility for our work in the country, and he had to sign my work documents. There was another minister who was a Shilluk, and we paid him a courtesy call. I learned from that visit that if a Sudanese does not shake hands with you when you come calling, he is in a VERY bad mood and you had better watch your step.

Finally, on February 17, I arrived in Malakal. The Director of Literacy, John H., came along to get me set up. David, the Sudanese Director of the Institute of Regional Languages (IRL), which sponsored us, also came to explain my work to the various officials in Upper Nile since we had not yet worked that far north. We traveled in a Cessna plane with Skip as the pilot. The plan was to visit officials in Malakal to inform them about my work to help develop the Shilluk language, and then eventually to get to the village where I would live, and where an American couple, Bill and Lois, already lived. We planned to spend the night at their place and get me set up. The next day, the pilot and the two directors would head back to Juba. I sent my belongings ahead in a lorry (large truck), as they would not have fit on the plane.

The White Nile as it flows
through Shilluk country

As we flew over the area which was to be my home, it was like seeing a whole new world. The landscape was flat and the White Nile and Sobat rivers twisted and turned like snakes through the land. Huge marshes contained papyrus reeds growing along the sides of the river. Herons, egrets, and storks skimmed the water's surface in search of fish. A description of this land is found in the Bible, in Isaiah 18:1-2 (NIV): "Woe to the land of whirring wings along the rivers of Cush, which sends envoys by sea in papyrus boats over the water. Go, swift messengers, to a people tall and smooth-skinned, to a people feared far and wide, an aggressive nation of strange speech, whose land is divided by rivers." Not much seemed to have changed from the time that was written.

As I listened to the conversations between David and the Sudanese officials, I was quite interested in seeing which words were borrowed from English and which were Arabic. They assumed that I didn't know any Arabic, and I didn't enlighten them, so they spoke freely about buying fuel on the *suuq aswad* (black market). In 1983, trading on the black market was about the only way to get fuel. We also met other important people in the community.

At one point, the official we were visiting asked if we had arranged an appointment with a particular person. "No," we answered. "Oh, let me do that for you!" and he reached behind his desk for a telephone. I looked at John H, and he looked at me.

"Do they have telephones here?"

I replied, "Well, they must have. He's talking on one!"

After a year in Khartoum without a working phone and six weeks in Juba without even seeing a phone, it was quite novel to be reminded of how helpful this marvelous invention could be!

Well before I arrived in Juba, our office had been housed in a government building which had a telephone. It worked, sometimes—usually when it was a wrong number. But when anyone wanted to make a call, it didn't work. It became such an irritation that the boss finally jerked the cord out of the wall and stuck the phone in a drawer. So much for communication in Juba.

We contacted several local agencies in the area to ensure they were willing to deliver mail and supplies. Then we headed for the village of Doleib Hill. Bill and Lois lived at a small Bible school there. The government officials decided that since the more educated Shilluks lived near the Bible school, Doleib Hill would be the best place for me to learn the Shilluk language.

We didn't drive from Malakal to Doleib Hill; we flew. It isn't that far, but we didn't have a car. It was also easier to have the plane closer when the others left the next day.

Malakal's airport was small, but the airstrip at the Sobat site, only a few miles from Doleib Hill, was even smaller. It served the headquarters of a French company which was digging a huge canal to divert some of the water from the White Nile before it reached the *sudd* (swamps), where much of it evaporated. Preventing its flow into the swamps would allow more water to reach Khartoum and, eventually, Egypt, which is desperate for all the water it can get. Naturally, the Egyptian government strongly supported this project. The company's specially designed digger had started at the Sobat site (where the Sobat River joins the White Nile) and was "eating" its way south. The plane landed here for my first trip to my village home.

As I stood near the high grass on the edge of the landing strip, waiting for Skip to close up the plane for the night, two Shilluk men walked past me. They were tall, at least six feet eight inches, and slim. They wore bright-pink cloths tied over their left shoulders and carried long hunting spears. What caught my attention was that these two men were holding hands. I quickly realized that things were very different here, and I was going to have a lot to get used to. It was common throughout Sudan for men to hold hands. It just meant they were friends. In Sudan, it was inappropriate for a man and a woman to hold hands in public, even if they were married. The pink *lawø* (cloths) are traditional for Shilluk men. Women wear a similar cloth, but usually of a darker color, and tie it on the right shoulder instead of on the left. Men need to keep their spear arms free from encumbrances. You never know if you will meet a wild animal on the way home.

Shilluk man in pink *lawø* with
his spear

We traveled by boat to get to the school compound, where Pastor Michael greeted us warmly. He was the principal of the Bible school and belonged to the Nuer language group. He helped us settle in and explained that our hosts, Bill and Lois, would be back later in the evening.

We had a quick tour before sunset. Doleib Hill was hardly a hill at all since it rose all of twenty-five feet above the level of the river. You had to be off it to know it was a hill. Everything in Shilluk country was pretty flat, as is much of southern Sudan. This hill was artificially created by people building structures in one place. As this building aged, they tore it down and built on top of the rubble. Gradually, a small hill developed. The Sobat River flows to the west of the compound, and it was lovely to watch the sun setting over the river with egrets and herons flying past and the outline of a graceful ostrich standing near the water's edge.

Sunset in Shilluk Land

When Bill and Lois arrived, we found that there couldn't be better folks to stay with or live near. They had "been around the block" a few times and guided me through my early days. They were welcoming and opened their home and their hearts. Lois seemed to love everyone and, as a result, everyone loved her. She is "mama" to thousands, I'm sure.

Love,

L

———

Dear Harriet,

My first night in the village passed peacefully. In the morning, we got a tour of the Bible school from Bill. He suggested I might want to live in a small, corrugated iron building between their house and the river. We had a look. The building had a wooden frame and two floors, one room up and one room down, with a rickety staircase leading to the upper floor. Instead of glass in the windows, a flap made of metal and wood covered the window openings. The flaps were hinged at the top. To open it, I had to push it out from the bottom and prop it open with a stick. To close, just remove the stick. Wooden two-by-fours with sizable gaps between them formed the upstairs floor. I could see the ground floor, and the dirt from any sweeping upstairs would quickly end up downstairs. Bill suggested putting a long-drop toilet outside. The house stood beneath a sausage tree, so called for its huge leaves and fruit that resemble long sausages hanging down. It was shaded from the direct sun for most of the day, so it might not be too hot. In a moment of weakness, I agreed to move there.

John H put up my solar panel and set up my solar system of lights and fans at strategic spots in the house. Bill and Lois used kerosene lamps, but Bill was at the forefront of sustainable technology. They had a "well" near the house where employees put cow manure and chicken droppings. The methane gas from the decomposing materials provided enough fuel for a few hours for lights and cooking. It was quite a recycling project! They could pipe water into my house, as there was already a water system in the compound. They just had to add my section to the existing setup.

Having set me up with lights, a shortwave radio, plans for water, and a loo, John H., David, and Skip returned to Juba. I had started my journey to this place in 1979, and in 1983, I had arrived! It had been a long and challenging trip. At last, I could start learning an African language and finding out about this amazing group of people. They had lived in what seemed to be the middle of nowhere for centuries. If they could live there, so could I.

While my house and long-drop were sorted out, Bill and Lois let me stay with them. Col, their Shilluk cook, arrived early in the morning. Mornings started with a cup of tea or coffee, and then we all started to work. At about 9:00 a.m., the cook served breakfast. My favorite meal was durra porridge. It doesn't sound all that wonderful, but it was. The grains of roasted durra, also known as millet, were boiled for some time. It was almost a chocolate color but tasted very healthy, especially with some brown sugar on it. The main meal of the day was lunch and was served about 2:00. Once the meal was ready and the kitchen cleaned, the cook went home. For supper, we were on our own for a lighter meal.

My specific job was to learn the language and then figure out why the Shilluk people were having trouble reading the books available in their language. Work to write the Shilluk language had begun some 80 years before by a German professor, Diedrich Westermann. After spending three months learning the Shilluk language, he wrote a two-volume tome on the grammar of the language, the culture, and some stories. He published the work in

1912. Years later, Father Kohnen completed a remarkable grammar of the language and published it in 1933. Knowing these men had come to this out-of-the-way place, worked there, and accomplished so much inspired awe, and still does.

Another amazing man was J. A. Heasty, who worked at Doleib Hill where I was living. He was a pastor and teacher, but in the course of his work to communicate with the Shilluk, he wrote a dictionary, Shilluk-English and English-Shilluk, in 1937.

The last major contributor to write about the Shilluk language was Prof. Archie Tucker from England. He and Margaret Bryan collaborated on writing about nearly every language in Africa, or so it seemed. Tucker traveled to Africa and collected immense amounts of data while Margaret Bryan stayed in England and helped sort it all out when Tucker returned. Together, in 1966, they published a book titled *The Non-Bantu Languages of Eastern Africa*. This work and Tucker's description of *The Verb in Shilluk*, published in 1955, completed all the information available in the literature.

So, I was not without resources to help me prepare for my first language-learning session with Obyec, Paul Akic, and Kwal Col. These three gentlemen offered to work without salary for the benefit of the Shilluk people. Impressed by their commitment, I planned to "encourage" them along in return for their help. We started work on February 23, meeting for an hour and a half a day. I took notes, asked questions, and listened to them say the same words repeatedly. I twisted my tongue in knots, trying to make my words sound like theirs.

The Shilluk people have a distinctive tribal marking called *thay wij*. Many Shilluks have a row of bumps across the forehead just above the eyebrows. Some bumps are very large and pointed; others are flat and not very prominent. I asked how they created this scarring and, upon hearing the process, assured my informant that I did NOT want to become a Shilluk.

Close-up of our cook who had the tribal markings
(*thay wij*)

During puberty, both girls and boys are identified as members of the Shilluk tribe. (The Sudanese do not find the word "tribe" offensive, though some other Africans do. Therefore, I will occasionally use this term since it is how the Sudanese describe themselves.) Someone inserts a curved fishhook into the skin on the forehead and pulls the skin away from the skull. Then they use a sharp knife to cut off the end of the flesh where the hook is. They repeat this process across the forehead, in about ten or more places. They rub ashes into the wounds so they will scar. The first scarring is usually flat, but they can repeat the whole process until the scars stand up in a point an eighth to a quarter-inch high, or should I say long. Anyway, you get the idea. Several generations ago, they made two rows of scars across the forehead. During this entire process, the boy or girl should never cry out or show they are in pain. If they do, they are deemed to be cowards and no one will want to marry them. Nothing like a critical audience to up the pressure!

The Dinka and Nuer have a different initiation rite. The teen lies on his or her back while an elder pulls a hot spear across the forehead in six straight lines. I understand the cuts are so deep that they can mark the skull. They only have to endure this torture once, but again without showing they feel pain. No anesthetics are used!

These marks identify their tribal affiliation. In battle, where people look alike and few wear any clothes, marks on the face identify friend from foe.

Love,

L

————————

Dear Harriet,

It didn't take long for my little metal house to become claustrophobic! Trying to decide where I would put my waterbed became a problem because of the weight, and the flooring upstairs didn't seem too strong.

Waterbeds, with no heater, were ideal for the climate in southern Sudan. The cool water made sleeping possible in the very hot weather.

After only a few days, I decided that living in a nearby tukul (mud house with a grass roof) would be a better choice. Most tukuls are round huts with grass roofs, but this one was rectangular. The three rooms served as a living room, bedroom, and kitchen with a screened-in breezeway off the bedroom and kitchen. With a long-drop toilet and shower dug next door, my needs were met. The placement of a Shilluk-style grass fence around the yard defined the compound. I fell in love with the place and eagerly awaited its completion so that I could move in. But it took a couple of weeks before that happened. We moved my solar equipment and radio, but most importantly, a second toilet had to be dug. Long-drops are approximately ten feet deep in hard clay soil. The man who dug both holes just loved his work. He worked from early in the morning until late in the afternoon. After a short time, I couldn't see him, only spades-full of dirt flying out of the deepening hole.

Leoma outside her home in Doleib Hill

We drove into Malakal, an hour-long journey by land, to shop for food and order furniture. The only furniture I brought was made by my Uncle Clyde. He created two lovely cedar chests with removable shelves for ease of packing. When I got to my final destination, I adjusted the shelves and used the chests to store my kitchen things or my personal things. One side opened to provide a desk or work area. Each chest rested on a cedar table wide enough to give extra support to the side of the chest that opened. Everything else, including chairs and the sideboards for my waterbed, had to be made locally.

Jimmy, the man in charge of getting my house ready, used his initiative to get a seat made for my long-drop. He kept it a secret until the concrete cover for the large hole was in place. Finally, the day came. He proudly led Lois, Bill, and me to the door and let me open it to see his creation. Wow! A throne fit for a queen! A very large queen…. The opening in the seat was large enough for me to fall through, but otherwise, it was splendid. I believe we got a regular toilet seat to use over the opening, which provided more support in critical places, and it worked well. Jimmy created a lid that fit over the seat to keep the smell from wafting out. The lid covered the hole and sported a long, perpendicular stick for lifting it off or putting it on. That stick added to the overall effect, and I smiled every time I saw it.

It took several weeks for my furniture to arrive, so by the time I moved into my new house, I had furniture as well. I enjoyed lying on my waterbed in the afternoons, looking up at the golden grass beautifully woven into the supporting poles on my roof. I didn't know if it would keep out the rain, but it was cool and peaceful. They installed my solar lighting on the beams about ten feet off the ground. That gave plenty of light for my early morning study sessions. I found it easier to study in the cool of the morning and do busy work in the hotter part of the day. It was time for a rest on my waterbed after lunch. In the late afternoon, I visited neighbors or worked for another hour or so.

At night, Lois and Bill and I ate a light supper together. Afterwards, we listened to a sermon from a cassette tape or talked over the events of the day. The noisy birds and the ever-present fruit bats kept us entertained. The stars were magnificent, as there was no light pollution to mar the view. One evening, as I looked up at the stars, the thought came to me that it looked as though someone had spilled milk up there. The words rang a distant bell: milk → milky → Milky Way! So that's what they were talking about.

I arrived in the dry season, but the rainy season was on the way. Bill and Lois advised me to stockpile food for the rainy season since it was difficult to travel when the road was wet. The hard-packed clay soil, which provided lots of washboard surfaces to ride on when dry, turned into a gooey, slick mess when the rains came, and even large lorries got stuck until things dried out. Any travel to Malakal during the rains had to be done by motorboat. The trip to Malakal by water took about an hour as the river flowed north. However, the trip back against the current could take up to three hours. The boat's motor probably had 3 HP. I didn't want to be out in the sun that long in an open aluminum fishing boat.

Going by road to Malakal was still an endurance contest. After the bumpy ride, we headed for the market for shopping and completed the errands on our lists. We had nothing to drink or eat or a chance to relieve ourselves for the whole day. There was not even a chance to sit down and rest. A few expatriates lived in Malakal, and by mid-afternoon, we stopped to visit one household where we enjoyed water, a loo, and a cup of tea.

One fine day, we visited our neighbors at the Sobat site, where they were digging the canal. This French company was a major source of employment for the local population. The people we visited were French, but they spoke some English. The employees from France were on a regular rotation. They worked long hours for six weeks and then returned home to France for a month before coming back again. The pay was generous, and the company flew in many wonderful things, like wine and cheese. We got a sample. They lived in shipping containers converted into houses. The company's big generator kept them supplied with electricity for lights, air conditioners and refrigerators. At Doleib Hill, we used a kerosene fridge, which wasn't particularly efficient and needed frequent maintenance just to stay operational. So, drinking COLD water from a real electric refrigerator was a novel treat.

Bill told me of a Shilluk man who had several wives. Each wife took responsibility for a different part of his holdings. One wife and her children looked after the cattle, another cared for the farm, another tended the fruit trees. Reportedly, he was looking for a fourth wife to run an ice cream stand at the Sobat site. Bill teased me, saying if he found out I knew how to make ice cream, I could be in the running for his next bride.

Oh, goody! I thought.

Having learned I was single, several locals made inquiries to see if I was open to marrying an African. The most common way to find out was to send an envoy to the prospective bride. The envoy asked the tricky questions and if the response was favorable, then the man in question would come calling. If the envoy received a negative response, that was the end of it and no one lost face. In Shilluk country, the usual bride price was ten cows and a variable number of sheep and goats. The bride's family could ask for a canoe. I heard this request was unpopular with grooms because they only found the wood for the canoe in Dinka or Nuer country. The Shilluk often fight with the Dinka and the Nuer, so it was tricky to get your tree, make your canoe, and get out again without being spotted. Bill said most canoes were flown in from Ethiopia.

My things were all unpacked by March 24, and I invited Bill and Lois over for supper. I even made bread, though it was only fit to feed to the chickens. Life was how I had imagined it and I felt content. It's funny how much you can change in the course of a year. As I unpacked my things, I realized I had no teapot! How could I not have a teapot? I had never used a teapot before coming to Africa. After a year and a half in Africa, I couldn't live without one. I added that to my market list!

By March 30, I had a virus of some sort. The thermometer read 106.3, and that was BEFORE I put it in my mouth. It wouldn't shake down any further until it cooled off in the evening. I decided the country had a fever, and I needed to go to bed until we both felt better.

One day, I joined Bill and Lois for lunch. While waiting to eat, I meditated on how it was possible to survive in such heat. I was glad that wearing sundresses didn't offend anyone. Looking out the window, I saw one of the employees preparing to leave for the day. He pulled a wooly hat onto his head and rolled it up above his ears. After that he put on his *lawø*, the pink cloth, and adjusted it until it felt right. Finally, he took his green cardigan and threw it back over his shoulders, tying the arms together and draping them over his chest. He picked up his spear and started on his way home. I observed this procedure in amazement. I exclaimed to Lois, "How on earth can he stand to wear a wooly hat and that sweater?!?"

With years of experience behind her, she replied, "How will anyone know he has them if he doesn't wear them?" What more can you say?

When she and Bill first arrived in Upper Nile province, most local people wore no clothes, just strings of beads. A well-meaning person sent a shipment of white T-shirts which were distributed to the local people. Many of the recipients turned up wearing the T-shirts, but nothing else. That white shirt ended at an awkward place and Lois said she had to take care where her eyes wandered.

One evening, as Bill and Lois and I sat in my compound listening to a tape, I saw something moving in my doorway. I went over and found a small snake. It was small enough that I could squish its head with my flip-flops, so I did. A search the next morning revealed a few more little ones. They turned out to be poisonous enough to kill cattle, and the babies are more venomous than the adults. From then on, I was careful to have a flashlight handy when I got out of bed at night. Bill and Lois reminded me to be extra cautious during the rainy season, as snakes don't like to get wet. When the land around the hill got soggy, they headed for higher ground, and thus to Doleib Hill. That gave me pause, and I was not so sure I was looking forward to the rainy season.

All of this may sound fun, and it was. But culture stress was building up. I had been through the Cameroon orientation course, followed by a year in Khartoum getting to understand and relate to Arab culture, six weeks in Juba, learning to adapt to southern Sudanese culture, and now to Shilluk country, where everything was different yet again. Looking at the river one evening, I realized I had been in Africa for a year and a half with no vacation. My stress level had just about peaked, and I decided a brief break in a European environment was what I needed. Many of my English friends from Khartoum had returned to England, so it would be nice to visit them. Once I felt refreshed and renewed and less stressed, I could return to Doleib Hill and continue my work.

Love,

L

———

Dear Harriet,

In April, while planning my vacation, I realized I had no hard currency and no passport. My passport remained in Juba for the office staff to do the necessary immigration work. So, I asked the office in Juba to send me various documents: an exit/re-entry visa, a plane ticket from Malakal to Khartoum and on to the U.K., and U.S. dollars. I hoped to leave at the beginning of May. We expected only one flight to arrive in Malakal before May, and those things needed to be on it. Then I wrote a bunch of letters to the people I expected to visit. Having prepared for my vacation, I got back to work.

In the afternoon, I enjoyed going to the river to watch the children. They took baths, swam, and had a good time. Shilluks prefer to live along the river, and thus teach their children to swim at an early age. Historically, crocodiles posed more of a problem, but I saw nothing but a monitor lizard. Water lilies have choked up the river. Supposedly, the wife of an early explorer brought a water lily out to Sudan or Egypt and put it in the Nile. There are now millions of them. They have become a menace to boats. When the water level drops, you can practically walk across the Nile on lily pads.

People slept soon after sunset unless there was a dance. The night should be quiet, but it wasn't. The noises came from animals. Crickets chirped and the ibis shrieked, even at night. Then there were the fruit bats. Fruit bats are large as bats go and, as the name implies, they live on fruit. They gorged on the grape-sized fruit of the neem trees. Whenever I woke in the night, they were chomping, slurping, and gulping them down.

I never saw the lovely mats or pots or beadwork that were in people's homes at the market. I asked my teachers, and they explained Shilluks do not believe in selling things in the market. If they put items out for sale, they considered it enslaving themselves to others, and that was unacceptable. Instead, I should go to the craft person and order what I wanted. That way, they felt honored. They told the story of an army officer whose mother wanted to keep busy. She began preparing food and sold it in the market in Malakal. Well! This officer became the focus of a song that accused him of not taking proper care of his mother. Unfortunately for him, this critical song became very popular for dancing. Sometimes fights broke out when it was sung in the presence of his extended family, who took offense. I learned that one effective way to control behavior is to "sing songs about you."

Another taboo involved owning or using a donkey. I never understood why that was a bad thing. Another common practice is that Shilluks don't spend the night in the town, but always return to their village to sleep.

I didn't visit my Shilluk neighbors. My language skills were inadequate, and I needed to gain control of life in small bits. Dealing with life in my new house and preparing for the unknowns of the rainy season kept me occupied. Many visitors came, so a sense of isolation didn't drive me to visit. But I wanted to see the traditional dances regularly held during that time of year. Sadly, the Shilluk king had ordered his house rebuilt and no dances could take place until they finished.

Before I knew it, Easter was upon us. I learned it was a tradition on Easter Monday for expatriates in Malakal and the surrounding area to come to Doleib Hill for a potluck lunch. We were in charge of the ice cream. We expected fifteen to twenty people, so we needed lots of ice cream and we only had the old kerosene fridge. Lois had the task well in hand. She collected milk for several days and began the slow process of freezing ice. It took two days to freeze two or three trays of ice. The day before the event, Bill cooked the ice cream ingredients and started cooling it enough that the ice we had available would freeze it into ice cream. They placed the large bowl of ice cream mix in the refrigerator and no one opened the door for any reason short of an emergency.

Easter Monday morning there was a sort of emergency. Someone had shot a hippo near the Sobat site, and meat was available for sale. Meat was a rare commodity, and hippo meat was tender. Bill bought a large hunk of meat and put it on a plate in the fridge. He planned to deal with it after the guests had gone.

The guests arrived, and we got acquainted. Lois informed Bill to get moving with the ice cream freezer, the old-fashioned hand-crank variety. So, he removed the ice cream mixture and prepared to put it in the freezing cylinder. At that point, he noticed something pink floating on the top. *Had he put* kerkedeh *(hibiscus) in the ice cream?* he wondered. No, he couldn't remember doing that. Just as he started to stir it together, the realization dawned on him that the ice cream mixture had been sitting under the plate of hippo meat. He checked and sure enough, blood from the hippo meat had filled the plate and dripped into the ice cream mix. UGH!

What to do now? he wondered. He told Lois, and she nearly fainted from the thought. But in good explorer tradition, he carefully dipped out the blood and finished making the ice cream. He threatened to tell everyone there was hippo blood in the ice cream, and she threatened him if he did! Everyone ate it, although Lois, Bill, and I had somewhat less than everyone else. No one got sick, and no one was the wiser.

The other memorable event during this time was a mini-conference that Bill organized. He invited several people from Khartoum to discuss education-by-extension courses he was writing. A woman named Suad attended, but Bill loved to aggravate her by calling her Sauud (a wad of chewing tobacco). She was an important figure in the Evangelical (Presbyterian) Church and was referred to as *Ummana* (our mother). She stayed with me during the conference, and it challenged me to speak Arabic because she didn't understand English. The conference was held in Arabic. Ummana wore black, most of it polyester. She kept her head covered and her long-sleeved dress extended from up around her neck to her feet. I still don't know how she coped with the heat in that outfit. She had lived many years dressed like that, so I guess she was used to it. She loved to joke around and even laughed at Bill for calling her a "wad of chewing tobacco"!

My ticket, money and passport with the needed stamps arrived. When I returned from vacationing in England, I expected to attend a special linguistics workshop with a renowned phonetician, Prof. Peter Ladefoged. Since the workshop was in Juba, it made more sense to travel through Nairobi. We were going to work on Shilluk vowels during the workshop, so I sent my language data on cassette tapes and paper. I sent rolls of film and a couple of sun dresses to Juba along with my language notes to lighten my load. I expected England to be colder than Juba and wanted to have a few cool, cotton dresses to wear during the workshop.

The day before I left for Khartoum, we drove into Malakal, where I spent the night. I wanted to get to the airport on time. The only flight available was on Sudan Airways, and you've previously heard stories about them! The schedule showed it going from Khartoum to Malakal to Wau. The return journey should be the reverse. My hostesses said people had planned to go to Khartoum on this flight the previous week. When the plane came in from the capital, airport authorities assured everyone that it would fly as planned. But the pilot had other ideas. A few prospective travelers discovered the pilot intended to fly back to Khartoum from Wau and not return to Malakal. Those few threw their luggage over the barrier and forced their way onto the plane. It took off and went to Wau, then went straight back to Khartoum. Anyone who waited for it to return to Malakal was still waiting.

We headed to the airport when the plane arrived to see if the pilot planned to come back. Everyone agreed he would, and in fact, he followed the schedule that day. While waiting at the airport, I met a handsome, educated Shilluk man who taught in Tonga, the far west side of the Shilluk territory. We talked about my plans and he sounded very interested in helping me develop literacy materials in the language. I suggested he get transferred to Doleib Hill and we could work together when I returned. I left, encouraged that things were looking up.

It felt strange returning to Khartoum after these few months. It was still hot and people were friendly, but it was no longer where I belonged. That night I slept on the guesthouse veranda, trying to stay cool. The next night I flew to England for a month of being cold, eating pastries, reveling in green grass and trees, and seeing rain for the first time in roughly a year. I'd forgotten that it could rain, but England reminded me in short order.

Love,

L

Dear Harriet,

The Sudanese rarely tell anyone when they are planning a trip, and I've figured out why. As soon as you are going somewhere, it implies that you have money. If you have money, then maybe you can bring them something. My list of requests when leaving the village was fairly lengthy and included raincoats for the teachers I worked with. I'll never forget the look on the English salesman's face when I asked him if they sold any pink raincoats for men. They didn't. I returned via Nairobi with two suitcases full of stuff for other people.

Sudan Airways was not flying between Juba and Nairobi in June, so Prof. Peter and I flew on a small plane to Juba. It was awe-inspiring to travel with such a well-known person. I had even studied his books during my linguistics courses. He spent part of the journey reading a message from his wife that she spoke and then printed out the sound waves. He knew her voice well enough to figure out the message just from looking at the waveforms. Wow! I had never heard of that being done.

We arrived in Juba and I settled into the guesthouse. My clothes and tape recorder and language notes had arrived, but none of my photos. I thought I'd have plenty more where those came from. Our workshop lasted two weeks and during that time, my world fell apart.

During my adjustment to Sudan, I hadn't noticed the discontent growing among the southerners. Perhaps it was my failure to read the history of Sudan and to come to grips with the issues surrounding the seventeen-year civil war. That war had resolved only ten years before my arrival. True, I knew how Sudan gained its independence from Egypt and Britain on January 1, 1956. But I failed to read and understand that afterward, there was a mutiny involving southerners. The leaders of the mutiny became the core of the rebel movement known as Anya Nya (a name derived from a poison used in the Madi area).

In 1963, a more formal civil war started between the northern government and the Anya Nya. The poorly equipped Anya Nya had the advantage of knowing the territory and being able to fight a guerilla-style war. They were highly motivated, since they had little to lose. Many complex reasons provoked the fighting. But the reason that affected me was a push by the northern government to make Arabic the country's primary language and, along with that, Islam as the state religion. The sixty or so language groups in the south wanted to keep their languages, culture, and religions and to continue education in English instead of Arabic. Most southerners followed traditional faiths that venerated the ances- tor spirits, although a small percentage were Christians.

The Anglo-Egyptian Condominium government, which ruled until 1956, encouraged missionaries to work in various parts of the south. Much of their work focused on writing grammars of the local (vernacular) languages and then producing literacy materials to make education more accessible for a non-literate population. But I learned that in 1962, the central government "blamed the missionaries for inciting southern hostility."[3] The Missionary Societies Act controlled Christian missionary activity and in 1964 led to the expulsion of all Christian missionaries working in southern Sudan. In that same year, southern Sudanese began fleeing the country; Uganda reported receiving 60,000 refugees.

Stories of the war still abounded. The northern government, I was told, had banned vernacular-language books, and made possession of such materials a capital offense. Someone in Doleib Hill told me he saw the local school burned to the ground, along with stores containing the Shilluk books. It was hard to find the old books when I arrived.

By 1971, the government realized that it couldn't win the war by force, so negotiations resumed.[4] The northern government had gone through changes in leadership with the overthrow of General Aboud. The following year, President Nimeiri reached an agreement with the southerners on March 3. This agreement, known as the Addis Ababa Agreement, gave the south a great deal of autonomy and the right to develop literature in the local languages. The languages of instruction were to be English or Arabic. Based on these points, I could work in the country developing the writing system for the Shilluk language.

The agreement lasted for eleven years, but not all was peaceful. The language groups in Equatoria believed they had suffered the most

---

[3] Holt, P.M. and M.W. Daly, *The History of the Sudan* (London: Weidenfeld and Nicolson, Asia-Africa Series, 1979) 179.

[4] Ibid., 202.

during the war. They resented the Dinka, Nuer, and Shilluk peoples occupying so many of the important government positions. A campaign called *kokoro* (separation) began. Equatorians wanted the Nilotics (the Dinka, Nuer, and Shilluk) out of their region, and the northern government saw a chance to increase its influence.

In 1983, the central government unilaterally proclaimed re-division of the south. As I mentioned in my first letter to you, three states—Equatoria, Bahr el-Ghazal, and Upper Nile—made up the Southern Regional Government. The southern Sudanese were told to return to where they came from immediately. The re-division edict came out just as we were having our workshop in Juba.

There was a rebellion in the garrison at Bor, about 150 miles south of Malakal. This rebellion marked the beginning of the second civil war. We did not know the long-term consequences of the war. We just knew there was a problem, and it wasn't a small one.

I was planning my flight back to the village when word came from the director that he would not allow me to return to Doleib Hill. First, the rebellion might move north, and they didn't want me there. Second, if they had to send a plane and a pilot to evacuate me, it might risk not only my life but also the pilot's. I was supposed to stay in Juba.

When that news came, I found myself alone with my few clothes, my tape recorder, and language notes. I was hundreds of miles from my lovely home, new friends, and everything I had worked toward for years. I had no family, no things, and now no job because I could no longer live in the Shilluk area. I was stunned, and little anyone could say offered much comfort.

Love,

L

Dear Harriet,

When life hits you over the head, you still have to get up each morning and get through the day. People still talked to me and I guess I talked back. I ate a little but moped around a lot. Jill and others tried to cheer me up. They were going to a party at the French compound. The same company building the canal was also building a new airport in Juba. There was a get-together one evening. I agreed somewhat half-heartedly to go, mainly to get my mind off my dismal situation.

People lent me clothes since I only had a few items to wear. My losses weighed heavily on me, particularly the fact that I was supposed to look after myself, and everything I needed to do that with was in Doleib Hill. I guess I never realized how much my stuff contributed to my identity, a "you are what you have" mentality. It goes along with the "you are what you do" role model. I was stripped of both.

During those painful days, I prayed often. I asked God what to do and how to respond to these many losses. I felt God respond at last, but not as I expected. "Do you own your things or do your things own you?"

"What do you mean?"

"If you own your things, you can give them up. But if they own you, then you can't give them up. Which is it?"

Now there's a question for you! I realized up to that point, my stuff owned me and that was not how I wanted to live my life. So, at that moment, I "owned" my stuff and could give it up. After all, I had God's promise that he would never leave me or forsake me. In Philippians 4:19, it says my God will meet all my needs according to his glorious riches in Christ Jesus. That being the case, God allowed me to experience this. He promised to take care of me, and I believed him. I relaxed. I still didn't know how it would work out, but I had complete confidence that it would. I attended the party and enjoyed myself and, after the party, had the best night's sleep for several days.

My problem didn't resolve immediately. After three days, the director decided I could fly up to Doleib Hill and get my stuff, but had to come right back to Juba. That wasn't the answer I wanted, but it was better than nothing. Skip, the pilot, and I made plans for the two-day journey. It was about five hours of flying time to Doleib Hill. He removed all but two seats on the plane, one for him and one for me. The rest of the space would be for my stuff on the return journey. I put all my gifts for my friends into one large suitcase and hauled it to the plane.

We left early in the morning. Skip made a contraption from a couple of scarves and a weighted can with a message in it. The message was dropped over Bill and Lois's house to tell them to pick us up at the "canal" landing site. Arriving near Doleib Hill, we circled Bill and Lois's compound and Skip threw the message out of the plane window as we passed over. The rushing wind ripped away one of the nice scarves, and I expect some Shilluk was soon wrapped up in it. Anyway, they waved they had seen it and we flew toward the landing site. Skip called the airport on the radio, but there was no answer. It turned out we were on different frequencies and we narrowly missed being shot down. After we landed, he secured the plane. It had been raining, and the ground was a mass of gooey, slick mud. Skip lugged the heavy suitcase for me, assuring me he would have the longest arms of any pilot alive by the time we reached the river.

The boat arrived, and we piled in. After another hour, we reached "home." It was very hard to tell Bill and Lois of the decision to leave, and even harder to explain it to the Shilluks. The teacher I had met when leaving for England turned up, ready to work, and was understandably upset to learn I was not staying. Nothing I said made it right. The location where the war began was far away. Why should I worry about a small thing? He was prepared to do important work. Why couldn't I stay? I wondered the same things. Bill and Lois weren't leaving! Why was I?

The teachers enjoyed their gifts. That was my one happy moment. I pulled the plug on my waterbed and started draining out the water.

The rains brought amazing changes to the area. Jacaranda trees were in full bloom with their huge red blossoms. The grass was high, and I imagined a snake waiting for me with every step. I wore my new Wellington boots, purchased in England for just such an occasion. The other small joy was sitting under the stars with Bill and Lois sharing ice cream. They had been preparing it for another occasion but let us share it instead. Bill kept apologizing that he didn't have any hippo blood to put in it!

As I went to sleep for the last time in my lovely house, I cried out again to God. "What should I take? How can I do this?"

In my mind, he gently whispered, "Take whatever you want, but know you will never see this place or anything you leave behind again."

"No!" I cried. "I don't want it to be that way!"

Then, in the silence of the night and through my tears of anguish, I felt Him say, "I know, but that is how it is going to be." I felt He was weeping with me for He, more than I, knew what suffering was coming. Unlike many of my Shilluk friends, I had the chance to take my things with me when I left home. I was spared the worst of the suffering.

In the morning, Skip assured me weight was not a problem. Space was the defining parameter. So, as tightly as I could, I packed the cedar boxes, the waterbed, and my little oven. Bill and Lois took the gas bottle because of size and possible leakage. I packed my books, clothes, pots, pans, and tools into as little space as possible. When I finished something, Skip hauled it out to the yard and lined it up as if it were on the plane. When I finished, we carried everything to the river and put it in the boat. It took a half hour to reach the company landing. The French company's Toyota truck took everything to the plane. It had to fit or be left behind on the landing strip.

While putting my belongings into the pickup, the company pilot helping us said he had packed many Cessna planes—not all of this would fit. I told him in no uncertain terms that it had to fit. We reached the plane and Skip did a wonderful job. I think there were six square inches of space left after everything was inside. We got in, the engines started, we taxied to the end of the runway, and the plane took off.

We flew south over the home I had just left and would not see again. The tears flowed and did not stop for weeks. Skip tried to make conversation but ended up handing me another Kleenex. When he thought I had regained control, he tentatively asked, "Where should I put your things when we get to Juba?" I answered with yet more sobs and tears, more Kleenex requests, and a long pause. He tried again, with the same result. We flew over the huge digger that was working its way south, creating the canal. It was so big I could still see it from the air. I cried over that, too. And so we traveled, Skip flying and me crying.

As we neared Juba, Skip tried to tell the controllers in the tower we were approaching to land. No answer. They were out for afternoon tea. He announced on the radio for planes in the area to be alert to our approach and, soon after, we were on the ground. He tried again to get an answer to his question regarding my things—in my house or in storage. More tears. I got out of the plane while he and some other men unloaded the contents onto a pickup. Skip put away the plane and checked in with the tower. The controllers had finished their tea and returned to work.

In the truck, Skip tried again to find out what to do when we arrived at the SIL compound. More tears. We drove a few kilometers and, as we entered the compound that was to be my temporary home, he tried again. More tears. He left the truck in the driveway with my stuff piled on it until I could finally tell him to put it in storage. We never spoke of that trip again. It was just too hard.

Love,

L

Chapter 6
Establishing a Life in Juba

Dear Harriet,

A few weeks after the evacuation, I moved to a one-bedroom apartment on the SIL compound. This area of Juba is called *sitta biyuut* (six houses). There were more than six houses, but perhaps when named, there were only six. The section next to ours was called *raajil maa fii* (there are no men). It leaves one wondering...

Life gradually righted itself. I had my stuff and my life. That was a lot to be thankful for. Some of my colleagues found it hard to understand why leaving the village traumatized me. After all, they lived in Juba and it was a nice place. I guess you had to be in my shoes to understand.

To make matters worse, just as I arrived, the Shilluks in Juba left for Malakal to follow the re-division policy. Having left thousands of Shilluks in Upper Nile, very few remained in Juba. Some were businessmen or those who had civilian jobs, but I didn't have a clue how to find them. My efforts to continue to work in this situation seemed impossible. Then I met an Acoli (pronounced a CHOLE - ee) man who worked for SIL, buying plane tickets, sorting out visas, and running errands. The Acoli are related linguistically to the

Shilluks. But just as I was about to give up, he offered to help me meet some Shilluks. In a few days, he told me of a Shilluk businessman who ran a tobacco company in town. We went off to meet Matthew. Matthew had another visitor in his office that day, a Catholic nun named Sister Theresa Nyathow. When I described what I wanted to do, she said, "I'm a teacher and I'm a Shilluk. We could work every day if we lived closer."

"I'll come get you. Where do you live?" And so began a very long friendship and working relationship.

Every afternoon, five days a week, I worked with Sister Theresa. We visited the few Shilluks who remained in Juba or we worked at my house for a couple of hours. I have many Sister Theresa stories. The point is, God kept his word. He gave me back my stuff and my work and I have lacked nothing that I needed.

Barbara came to teach at the Bible school at Doleib Hill and used my village home for a time. I struggled, knowing she was there and I wasn't. Within a few months, however, they had to evacuate, too, and lost nearly everything. Bill and Lois escaped on the back of a lorry. After that, the soldiers looted and burned the Bible school. By contrast, I was still using my gas cooker and the cedar chests. God was faithful, even though the experiences were painful.

Love,

L

———

Dear Harriet,

Just as I moved to Juba, another single colleague, Heather, moved to Juba from her village location for reasons similar to mine. She agreed to manage the guesthouse but needed a place to live. As I was the only other single woman with SIL in Juba, she moved in with me. Houses on the center were brick with cement floors. The roof was corrugated iron. The ceilings provided both a cooler house and a place for the local wildlife, like geckos and lizards. You may have seen ceiling tiles in offices with metal grids to hold them in place. Well, in Juba, wooden grids held large squares of Styrofoam in place. The Styrofoam was so light that when the wind blew, it dislodged and allowed for gaps. The lizards occasionally fell through the gaps.

Our one-bedroom place felt crowded, so when we learned a couple needed to live in our apartment, Heather and I found a new home a quarter mile from the center. The owner, a government official, was moving to Khartoum, and he was delighted to have *khawajaats* (foreigners) rent his house and generate income. It had three bedrooms, a large screened-in veranda, kitchen, pantry, and salon. The salon was the size of two rooms and usually served as a formal sitting room and dining room. It had a separate entrance and could be closed off from the rest of the house. There was one inside bathroom with a flush toilet, sink, and bathtub. Since we had to go through one of the bedrooms to get to the bathroom, we designated that bedroom as the guestroom. We turned the salon into a third bedroom and office. There were separate rooms for an outside shower and a second toilet. The shower room functioned fine, but the toilet? Well, it was supposed to be the "stand up" flush toilet, but the bottom had fallen out of the unit and it became a "short drop." May I add a *full* short drop?

As I was filling my waterbed, it got too full. So, our Sudanese assistant used the waterbed's excess water to wash away some remains in the short drop. The smell had been overwhelming, but his efforts helped. We avoided using it, but our Sudanese house help didn't mind.

The pantry was bigger than the kitchen and painted midnight blue. That was an unhelpful color when the power failed and I needed to find something. The light from the flashlight or kerosene lamp got swallowed up in the darkness of the blue. With only one tiny window high on the outside wall, there was not enough ventilation to use that room as a kitchen. The one feature defining any room as "the kitchen" in a Sudanese home is the sink. There were no cupboards or shelves, just a sink. Most Sudanese women sit on a small *banbur* (footstool) and work on a grass mat on the floor. That way, they aren't working in the dirt or, in this case, on a bare concrete floor. Two large windows had screens and wooden shutters. Without bars on the windows, we closed the shutters each night before going to bed.

The screened-in veranda was the central gathering place. It was L-shaped, with the door to the kitchen on the short end of the L. We used that end for our dining room and the long side for our sitting room. Two bedrooms opened off the sitting room, mine being one of them. They were spacious (especially since I had little furniture), with ceilings ten feet high and made of plywood. I much preferred plywood to the Styrofoam ceilings used in the center's houses. At least the plywood was nailed down and didn't move when the wind blew. My room had two large, screened windows, but without glass. I enjoyed watching my neighbors' compounds, which proved educational, but more about that later.

A small, screened enclosure served as a front porch and helped to keep the flies from following you inside the house. There was a concrete yard with an outside water tap, a large metal framework that held up the water tank, and a storage room containing the owner's possessions. A large gate opened onto a parking place.

Oh, yes, the shower room and short drop were just across from the kitchen windows!

They painted the rooms in typical Juba colors: geriatric green, Pepto Bismol pink, dust storm yellow and Juba blue. We counted four colors (including black marks around the door) in the sitting room alone. When the previous residents painted, they didn't always move the furniture. Now the room was empty. There was an outline of what furniture was there before. We had guessing games as to what each shape might have been. The family had children who left dirty handprints on the walls and facings of all the doors.

Our first task was to get the place painted. SIL employed several local workers, and we asked if any of them would paint. No, they couldn't paint, but they knew someone. The supervisor brought two men to do the work. They came with nothing but their ability; we furnished the paint, the brushes, the ladder, etc. The first day or two went well, and they were making progress. But one of them found two holes in the walls, one in the kitchen and another in the pantry. We knew that rats, not mice but rats, had made the holes and were living in the walls. The painter decided he couldn't paint a hole, so he blocked up each hole with stones and painted them. That worked for me.

One morning, the painters turned up three sheets to the wind. Heather was at the center and I was home alone supervising these guys, since we had moved our things into the house. One guy was doing strange things, and I became alarmed. We had no phone, so I jumped on my bicycle and rushed over to ask the supervisor what to do. He seemed unconcerned, and no one else took me seriously. I felt frustrated about that. I returned to the house and told the men to take the day off. "Come back when you feel better." Once I got them through the gate, I locked it.

That evening, Heather and I discussed how to handle the situation. We decided that if our male colleagues were not willing to take action, we would have to do it. We planned to leave the doors locked the next morning so the workers couldn't get in. It turned out that was the cultural thing to do. The men understood they had been fired. They returned to the supervisor for their pay. The supervisor was none too pleased with us, and even some of my colleagues acted as though we were overreacting.

But to this day, I don't want drunk painters in my house. Grudgingly, they found another painter to complete the job. The house was becoming a home.

Love,

L

Dear Harriet,

Once the painting was done, we needed to furnish the house. In Juba, we easily ordered furniture. Trees were plentiful, and carpentry was not a rare skill. We had wardrobes and kitchen cabinets made, and shelves for the pantry. Typical Sudanese chairs have wooden frames with armrests and thick cotton cushions to pad the wooden slats in the seat. We ordered six chairs, a coffee table, and several little side tables. Whenever guests came, we needed to serve them a glass of water and a cup of tea, placed on a small table within easy reach.

Hillene was returning to Juba after a brief break with her family in the Netherlands. We allocated her the bedroom next to mine, while Heather had the large salon at the end of the house. I had my room painted blue, but I left Hillene's room pink. The paint looked okay, and we had had more trouble with painters than my patience could tolerate. So, when she arrived, she cringed at the color, but it must have grown on her because she stopped complaining after a few months.

With furniture and painting completed, we next had to tackle the wildlife. We knew the rats were a problem. If we left food scraps in Tupperware containers overnight, the rats nibbled the lids until they came off and then helped themselves to the contents. Blocking up the holes didn't stop them, since they promptly pushed the stone out of the way. One rat ate the cement after we tried cementing up the holes. I expect that one died from the side effects of cement hardening into concrete in his stomach. One down, but how many to go? We considered poisoning them, but the neighborhood cats might eat the remains and die. Someone suggested using rat traps, but neither Heather nor I could face setting one, or worse, emptying it.

One night, I went into the kitchen to close the shutters. I had closed and bolted the first set and started on the second set when I noticed movement out of the corner of my eye. The electricity was off, and we did not have a solar light in that room, so it was tricky to see. I turned my flashlight in that direction, and lo and behold, there was a rat with its tail caught in the shutter's hinge. It jumped up, trying to get loose. My first thought was *OW! That must hurt!* I considered opening the shutter, but there was no way to do it without getting my hand near the teeth of a very annoyed rodent. No, release was not the answer.

I decided to hit it on the head with a long pole, but we didn't have one. I was frustrated by that. The only tool available was a hammer. For any animal rights activists who don't approve of killing animals, you were not around to consult during this crisis. Without giving it too much thought, I closed my eyes and repeatedly hit the rat with the hammer. Mercifully, it died after five or six blows. Once it was clearly dead, I opened the shutter and the six-inch-long body of the rat and its three-inch tail dropped onto the window ledge. I picked him up by the tail with a pair of pliers and threw him out onto the street for the local cats to enjoy. Two down, how many more to go?

Someone suggested putting out a tasty food treat mixed with cement and a dish of water close by. The rat would eat the cement, drink the water, and let nature take its course. No harm would come to the neighborhood animals. We tried it and got rid of one or two more. The rest must have died outside or decided it wasn't worth staying. We had won the battle of the rats.

Love,

L

Dear Harriet,

You may recall that Hillene and I had become acquainted when she stayed with me in Khartoum. After going home to the Netherlands for a visit, Hillene flew from Amsterdam via Nairobi to Juba. Getting to Juba proved considerably challenging. The Sudan Airways plane kept having problems. Either it didn't arrive from Khartoum to Nairobi, or once it reached Nairobi, it malfunctioned. Usually, the repairs required an overnight stay. Sometimes the repairs took a couple of days. There was a rumor that the pilot's girlfriend lived in Nairobi. Wanting to spend time with her, he made sure the plane "had a problem" regularly. Who knows? Hillene checked in and just before boarding, the plane "broke down" yet again. The passengers were put in a hotel at the airline's expense. During that time, Hillene met Big John, a Dutch-Canadian who was doing construction work in southern Sudan. He invited her to a party celebrating Canadian Thanksgiving at the Canadian Embassy and Hillene won one of the door prizes, a round-trip ticket from Kenya to England! The next day, the now-operational plane flew to Juba. Hillene took up residence with us and worked as the office manager.

Our house became known as the "Swinger House." I'm not sure why we got the name. Any single woman who needed a place to stay came to us. As single women, we attracted a fair number of single men who liked to come by for meals. We put the appetites of the single men to good use and began systematically inviting them for a meal. While eating, we laid out the rules of our competition. If he could repair the vertical blinds in this house so they worked, we would feed him one meal a day until all of them opened and closed correctly. Mike was the winner of this contest, and he ate with us for several weeks, repairing a set of blinds on each visit. Initially, the blinds stayed on one side of the window while the knotted pull cords hung in the middle of the window at eye level. By the time he finished, they pulled perfectly. Mike won not only many meals but also Hillene's heart. They have been married for thirty years and have three children.

Our lives took on a pattern. One person prepared a hot meal at lunch for the week, another baked bread, and the third shopped at the market. Hillene and Heather worked at the center, and I worked at the house in the morning. We ate our main meal about 2:00, while it was still light enough to see what we were eating. After a brief rest during the heat of the afternoon, I headed off in a car to pick up Sister Theresa. I rented the car for $.20 a kilometer. Sister Theresa's convent was on the other side of town.

Juba's main road was a large circle of fifteen kilometers (nine miles) of paved road. Sister Theresa and I lived at opposite points along it. So, I racked up thirty kilometers a day just in travel costs. It was worth every penny. Sister waited for me to arrive at 3:45 and we discussed the latest events of the war or her class at school or whatever until we reached the house. Then from 4:00 until 6:00 we worked on Shilluk: learning vocabulary, explaining culture, transcribing stories, conjugating verbs, and identifying singular and plural nouns. At 6:00, I took her home and returned home in time for the evening meal.

On one trip, the children on our street began calling out, as they often did, "*Khawaja, khawaja!*" (White person, white person!). Sister was in the car and shouted back, "*Ana khawaja?*" (Am I a white person?). To which they replied in Arabic, "No, no, Sister, we didn't mean you!"

Another afternoon, some small children were playing under my window. They got bored and wanted to get the *khawaja* to come to the window. They threw a small rubber ball against the screen of my window. To their shock, they didn't get the *khawaja* to the window, they got Sister Theresa! She called out to them, "Who threw the ball at the window?"

To this, a tiny voice replied, "Nobody!"

She laughed and asked, "Who is 'Nobody'?" The older of the two pointed guiltily at the smaller one. The children said how lucky the students at the Catholic school were because they could still attend school. The local schools had closed because of a teacher's strike. It said volumes about the value Sudanese children place on education.

Love,

L

Dear Harriet,

One day, we heard shouting in the neighborhood. We asked the neighbors what was happening. Of course, we imagined the worst: The rebels had invaded Juba. We were told *"haraka."*

Great. I knew the word for what was happening but didn't know what it meant. My dictionary listed words from English to Arabic, which worked well to find what I wanted to say. But it was useless to figure out what they were saying to me. Finally, I found out that it meant "fire" and sure enough, a fire had started in one house and spread to several others. Several families lost everything in this terrible accident.

Many houses in Juba were circular, with wattle and daub huts, upright poles and sticks filled in with mud. They then covered the dried mud with a patina of donkey or cow dung to protect the house from dissolving in the rains. They thatched roofs with sheaves of long grass that ended at a point and tied together at the top. Sometimes they added a decoration, such as a clay pot, over the top, but I'm unsure of its significance.

A compound has several huts or rooms surrounded by a fence. Each hut in a compound has a specific purpose. The husband entertains visitors in his room. If he has more than one wife, each wife has her own room. The older boys have their own room, as do the older girls. I'm not sure if they mixed the children of various wives since most of my friends had only one wife, and thus only one set of children. But children of relatives living with them stayed with the family's children. Then there was a kitchen. Sometimes the kitchen had a mud roof because of the fear of fire. Most women cooked with charcoal, which heightened the risk of catching something on fire. In a corner, preferably with a bamboo fence, was a shower and toilet. There may be a roof or not, depending on the family's affluence.

The ground throughout the compound was hard-packed earth that was swept each morning. It was rare to see a plant of any kind near houses, as that provided cover for snakes. No one wanted unseen snakes too near a house! Many of the nearby homes had no walls, so we could readily see the setup. Houses were in a circle, with the doors opening to the center. The family sat outside in the courtyard during afternoons and evenings, telling stories, entertaining visitors, drinking tea, and catching up with one another. There were few secrets in such a neighborhood.

Another day, Sister Theresa invited me to the home of a relative who lived in Juba. Our hostess welcomed us and brought two chairs out to a part of the compound shaded by the *tukul* (house). Once we sat down, she hurried off to bring us each a glass brimming with water. The brown color suggested it came straight out of the Nile (which it most likely did). I knew she possibly brought this water from a significant distance in a large jerry can balanced on her head. Perhaps she had paid for the water since she lived far from the Nile.

Knowing what this simple offering cost her, I felt compelled to drink at least a taste. Sister Theresa looked at me in surprise when I sipped it. She asked me quietly, after our hostess went into the house, if I wanted to drink the water since it was so dirty. I said I didn't but did not want to give offense. Sister Theresa took charge of the situation by pouring the water out onto the ground. She left the empty glasses on the table. We accepted our hostess's offer of a drink, and we didn't get sick. Sister Theresa taught me how to be a polite guest.

Love,

L

Dear Harriet,

Heather completed her contract and returned to the U.K. Soon after, Cathy came from the U.S. to replace her as part of our household. Cathy's arrival was even more eventful than most because no one knew Sudan Airways had changed their schedule of flights. Hillene and I were eating breakfast when the pickup truck arrived, and Cathy got out! We expected her in two or three days. The folks in Nairobi discovered that the flight schedule had changed from Monday to Saturday. Knowing how erratic flights to Juba could be, they suggested Cathy hop on the plane on Saturday. They didn't have a way to let us know she was on that flight. The Nairobi staff assured Cathy someone would hear the plane and come to the airport to check for a mailbag. Well, the plane didn't fly over the center, so no one went to check. She disembarked, proceeded through immigration and customs, and then stood around waiting, and waiting, and waiting. Cathy had no address. She couldn't get a taxi since there were no street names. So, she just waited.

Eventually, a helpful Sudanese with another nongovernmental organization (NGO) asked who she worked with. She told him and he roared off on his motorcycle to tell our office we had a passenger waiting at the airport. Within a half hour, she had been rescued, and all that before breakfast!

She moved into the salon Heather had vacated and soon noted all the lizards and geckos in her room. I guess I had grown used to being stared at by the wildlife. It was not unusual to be working and sense someone or something watching me. When I looked up, a lizard with an orange head might be standing on the wall staring at me. We would gaze at each other for a while until one of us got bored. Either I would go back to work or the lizard would chase after something to eat. Having lizards in the house kept down the plentiful fly and mosquito populations. Cathy, at least at the beginning, did not share these sentiments. It didn't take long to discover the shrew that visited, but more about that later.

These incidents with the bats, the flies, and the mosquitoes prompted Cathy to make a list of reasons why she ALWAYS used her mosquito net. Every week, she added another reason to the list.

I added to her list on one occasion. Paul, our industrious house help, was washing dishes as I prepared his breakfast. I opened the door of the cupboard and discovered what looked like a million swarming ants—huge black ants. They were in everything! They had invaded the entire cupboard with all the dishes, pots, pans, silverware, kitchen utensils—the lot! When we opened the door, they spilled out onto the floor. Ants in Africa can have a nasty bite. I hastened off to get my Wellington boots, purchased to protect me from snakes. Then Paul and I sprayed with insecticide and swept out the remains. By the time my housemates arrived home for lunch, we had buckets of ants and I was fit to be tied. It turns out they had both seen the ants earlier in the morning but left me to discover and deal with them. They were lucky they didn't get ants for lunch!

The other bane of our lives was the weevil! Juba seemed to have the perfect climate for growing weevils. It was nearly impossible to kill weevil larva. The milling process involves tremendous heat, but they come through it unscathed. Once the flour arrived in Juba, the hatching process began in only a matter of weeks. If we stored flour in the freezer, weevils didn't develop until we took it out. If we caught it before the weevils hatched, bay leaves were supposed to be a good deterrent. We also tried some kind of sulfur poison that we put on a cotton ball and taped to the inside of the canister that killed weevils. The vile odor suggested the weevils might not be its only targets.

If the weevil killers failed, the next line of defense became the sieve. Sieves varied significantly in quality. I had opted for one like my mother had used when I was growing up—a mesh screen with the wheel inside to push the flour through. I am not sure whether my mother's sieve was better made or the weevils were less abundant. However, this little sifter became known in our household as the "Weevil Decapitator." It squished the weevil against the screen and pushed it through in little bits so that it wasn't visible in the finished product. We decided that ten weevil feet per cup of flour was just enough to add a bit of protein, but not too much flavor.

If we ate weevilly bread, cakes, and cookies long enough, we got used to the taste and no longer noticed it. When we had guests who expressed disappointment and even outright shock, we realized we had exceeded the "ten feet" limit.

We acquired other sieves that worked more effectively at removing weevils. So, when we were invited to a White Elephant Christmas party, we knew what one of our presents would be: the Weevil Decapitator. I labeled it for what it was and wrapped it up. At that party, someone from the American Embassy in Khartoum attended. He got my present and was thrilled. He had needed a sieve for a long time. I tried to warn him, but he couldn't hear what I said over the joyful noises he was making for getting this wonderful sieve. All the best to him.

Weevils were one kind of problem, but sand was another. One batch of flour was full of grains of sand. There was no way to remove sand. One colleague suggested making the bread (which crunched with grit) and then toasting it until it was very crisp. Then he thought we wouldn't notice the grit. We decided the sand was too much, so we gave the flour to our Ugandan house help, who made beer out of it.

We controlled the weevils by freezing them in our freezer! Now all we needed to control were the ants, roaches, crickets and, of course, the shrew.

Love,

L

———

Dear Harriet,

Several women had come from up-country to attend a workshop. Several camped out in various rooms of our house. The purpose of the workshop was to decide which activities should be accomplished for our work to "finish." The new language program's director added several activities deemed to be necessary. As a result, many of the language teams no longer met the standards proposed. The week was filled with stressful discussions, and our visitors were ready to explode. At that crucial moment, a shadow made the mistake of appearing along the walls of the sitting room on its way to the kitchen and pantry.

"Shrew! I see a shrew!"

The chase was on. Alice and Wanda each grabbed a broom; Eileen got a basket. We chased that poor beast around the entire house, shrieking and shouting and bashing at it. The neighbors doubtless thought we had lost our minds or that we had a snake in the house. After a half hour of this stress-relieving shouting, the shrew made its escape under the salon door. I'm sure it was relieved to get outside, and we felt much better for having released our frustrations.

We watched for the shrew, as it came in regularly. It squeezed through a small gap under the back door of the salon. Then, it skirted the walls through the sitting room, and then made a dash through the kitchen into the pantry. Shrews are carnivorous, so it was after the insects that were after our food. On the whole, we didn't view them adversely. They look like a mouse except for the long nose. The Juba Arabic name for these animals is *nahar tawiil* (long nose). Cats won't touch them as they don't taste good, even to a cat. They have a strong odor. We tucked a towel under the door to discourage these nightly rounds, but the shrew just left a dirty mark on the towel as it slithered in each evening. One night, we had a large group of visitors sitting in the living room. The shrew reached the entrance to the living room, saw the people, and beat a retreat. It scooted out the back door, waiting until the group had gone. I guess it remembered our chasing and shouting.

I have never been one to kill animals and was relieved that the shrew continued to escape harm. That is, until I was awakened in the middle of the night to the sounds of *crunch, crunch, munch, munch*. I lay on my waterbed trying to work out what noise had aroused me from a deep sleep, while the smacking and slurping continued from behind the solar panel batteries. I found my flashlight and shone it in the corner. There was a shrew eating a cockroach. This posed a dilemma: Should I try to kill the shrew or leave it to eat another cockroach or two? I reasoned by the time I found something to kill it, it would be gone. So, I decided cockroaches were less desirable and wished the shrew would learn quieter table manners.

That decision held until I got out a pair of shoes that I had not worn in a while. Fortunately, I had wrapped them in plastic because the shrew used this plastic bag as its personal toilet. The stench was disgusting. I decided that the next time I saw the shrew, it was done for.

My housemates ignored any living thing in the house with more than two legs. They waited for me to find and deal with it. Since I worked at home, I got stuck with many of these unpleasant chores. On one occasion, I went into the pantry for something before I took Sister Theresa home. A supposedly empty milk tin was rattling on the floor as I walked in. When I investigated, things got still. As I walked away, the tin danced around on the floor again. Knowing my housemates' habits, I returned to the main room and asked, "Has anyone heard any strange sounds from a milk tin in the pantry today?"

"Oh, yes. We were just waiting for you to hear it," came the reply.

"What is the problem?" asked the ever-confident Sister Theresa.

We entered the pantry together and she took charge. She slammed the lid down on the tin and picked it up, shaking it vigorously. Liquid dripped on to the floor. Whatever was in the tin was scared or had been there a long time. She carried the tin outside and in one movement, took off the lid and slammed the tin's open end to the ground. She gave me my instructions. "When I lift the tin, if it goes that way, you step on it. If it comes my way, I'll get it. Ready?"

I nodded, but was sure that I wasn't and never would be. She picked up the tin and two shrews ran in opposite directions. She stomped on hers and in a moment, it was dead. For some reason, mine got away. She gently chided me about letting it escape, then picked up a stick, split it, retrieved the dead body, and threw it in the trash. I suspect the one I missed continued to raid the pantry for months afterwards.

We had well-built ceilings, but above the ceiling lay another problem: bats. Every night at sunset, they flew out of our house in a cloud in search of millions of mosquitoes, flies, and whatever insects they ate. During the day, they were hanging upside down in our rafters, sleeping and pooping. Guano, or bat dung, is a valued fertilizer. If it isn't holding down the ceiling, it's great. It was only a matter of time before a bat got mixed up and ended up inside the house.

One evening after I returned from taking Sister Theresa home, my "brave" housemates were again waiting for me to solve an animal problem. A bat was flying around, and they began shrieking and hid behind me as if I were the courageous one. The bat swooped here and there, trying to get outside. I suggested opening the door, but they feared more would fly in.

"What do you want me to do about it?"

Hillene offered me her squash racket and, just at that moment, the bat flew into my bedroom. They pushed me into my room with the racket and shut the door. You know, I couldn't hit the side of a barn with a shotgun, and I don't know how they thought I was going to hit a bat. It evaded many abortive swings, but the bat got tired and perched itself on the wall. In all honesty, I closed my eyes and swung the racket in the general direction of the bat. I looked up, but it wasn't there. I didn't see it flying around the room. It wasn't on the floor. Where had it gone? Then I looked at my waterbed and saw bat blood on my sheet. The bat had fallen into a corner of the frame. GROSS!

I opened the door and told my cowardly housemates to get rid of the thing and get that bat blood OFF my SHEETS!

Enough wild tales for today.

Love,

L

Dear Harriet,

Continuing with my little saga, I must tell you about Hillene. She worked as our office manager and always had significant stories to tell us over lunch. She regularly took people to the airport or picked them up, so she witnessed most of my Sudan Airways stories firsthand. Remember, we lived in a remote part of the world, and few people journeyed there by choice. Here are a few samples of what she saw at the airport.

Cows presented a big problem at the Juba airport. The Mundari and the Dinka peoples kept cattle and valued them highly. They used them as a bank account on the hoof. But when the need was great, they would sell one. Now and then, whether by accident or design, someone got the bright idea of herding their cattle onto the runway in front of an incoming plane. If the plane struck the animal and killed it, the owner had to be compensated for his loss. They pulled that trick when the Sudanese President's plane came in. He was not amused. It happened so often, pilots buzzed the airstrip to chase away the cattle before attempting to land. I doubt this issue is a regular problem at most international airports.

Cattle weren't the only hazard to the planes, though. After a small plane had landed, one of the airport workers saw a dik dik (small antelope) startled out of the brush by the noise. The worker saw it running across the tarmac, chased after it and caught it. I guess he had a good meal that night. At least it didn't get run over by the plane!

Sudan Airways, locally known as *"inshallah* (God willing) airways," had an excellent safety record. However, its commitment to promptness was less obvious. If we were planning to fly out of

Juba, we depended on hearing the plane approach, and then rushed to the airport. For weeks, the radio in the control tower was inoperable and there was no radio contact between the plane and the Juba airport. So, one of the private cargo companies provided a useful service by listening in on its radio to discover when the plane was on its way. Then the company sent its car around to collect the immigration officials and take them to the airport.

Once the officials arrived at the airport, everyone swung into action. The airport easily accommodated twenty-five passengers in the international wing. Unfortunately, more than twenty-five wanted to travel. Those of us planning to fly from Juba to Nairobi filled out our forms and had the passports stamped. Then we opened our suitcases for the customs officials and then had them taken outside to be loaded onto the plane. If we were lucky, we completed these processes before the plane from Khartoum came to a halt. We stood outside and watched the remaining happenings from a cooler distance outside the terminal. The Khartoum-to-Nairobi passengers had to exit the plane and collect their luggage to go through immigration and customs. Often, 100 people were on that plane, and all squeezed into that tiny space in the international wing, with temperatures in the upper 90s with sticky humidity. It was not a pleasant experience. It was worse if we, as the Juba passengers, got stuck in the middle of this muddle.

On one particular occasion, I was traveling to Nairobi. The plane was coming from London to Nairobi via Khartoum and Juba. It was a cheap flight, and many people had taken advantage of the low fares. They didn't know they would pay the difference in sweat and aggravation. That day, the Juba passengers were still being processed when the British people began their ordeal. Those innocents had expected to fly directly to Nairobi, not go through immigration and customs en route. "Where are your yellow fever and cholera injections? You are leaving Sudan. You must have these shots before you can enter Kenya!" the officials shouted. How many of those people, traveling for a brief vacation in Africa, expected to be stopped mid-journey and threatened with an injection? There was a lot of fast talking going on there.

Next came customs and the command, "Yes, you must open your suitcase." The flight from Khartoum to Juba was an internal flight, but Juba to Nairobi meant crossing an international border. It didn't matter that these people had come straight from England. The customs officer had to see inside their suitcases.

Amid this chaos, I saw one young woman, dressed in what appeared to be a clown suit (though I am sure it was the latest fashion). She pulled out a camera and took pictures of the airport and the various soldiers who were carrying AK-47 rifles. If there were ever a country paranoid about cameras, it is Sudan. Visitors narrowly avoided arrest and the confiscation of their cameras just for carrying them around (without ever taking a photo). NEVER take pictures at an airport anywhere in Africa. She was lucky to have only lost her film. After a stressful hour, we got on the plane and departed. What a relief.

I never realized how important it was to have a fire engine on the scene when a plane landed. Fire engines are at other major airports, but not so visible. When our organization's Cessna came in, a man pulled a large fire extinguisher on a trolley. He stood by the plane, watching carefully lest it should burst into flames. He guarded the plane until the pilot put it in the hangar or flew away.

When the jets came in, the fire engine came out to offer its protection. However, as I have learned from hard-earned experience, any necessity can create its own problems. On several occasions, the plane from Khartoum had to turn back for lack of a fire engine. Perhaps they couldn't find the key or there was no fuel, or it wouldn't start. Since the fire engine could not make it to the airfield, the jet wasn't allowed to land. If the Juba people found the key, or solved the problem later in the day, the plane might make a return journey. But I was never sure if they informed the passengers that it was returning. At least the trusty fireman was on hand to ward off any blazes.

On one occasion, the runway developed a large hole, which didn't interfere too much with planes landing. Departure was another matter. Hillene was present one day when the plane arrived from Khartoum. Juba's passengers added to the load, along with excess baggage and freight. The plane taxied to the end of the runway for departure. Engines revved; the plane moved, picking up speed, stopped, turned around and returned to the terminal. It was too heavy to lift off before the hole in the runway. The excess baggage and freight had to be removed.

Down to the end of the runway again. Power, movement, then STOP. It turned around and came back. The plane was still too heavy. All the luggage came off the plane.

Down to the end of the runway yet again. Power, movement, STOP. It turned around and came back. The plane was still too heavy. The hand luggage had to be removed. I think I would have gotten off the plane and stayed with my luggage. But I didn't have to make that decision. The plane was now light enough to be airborne before the hole. We heard the luggage followed three days later.

I'm reminded of an incident which happened in 1983. Sudan Airways acquired an old Aer Lingus plane and had it fixed up for service. On its maiden voyage, it took a full complement of passengers to Jeddah to begin their pilgrimage to Mecca. It returned empty except for the crew, but never arrived at the airport. The pilot reported that he got caught in a wind shear and the plane landed in the White Nile south of Khartoum. The undercarriage broke, along with one wing. Significantly, only one member of the crew suffered a broken leg. There were no other injuries. The plane is still there. The Sudanese make a joke about anything. The joke that made the rounds regarding this incident went, "Someone needed a new restaurant, and they are going to use the downed plane. The name of the restaurant will be The Nile Perch."

Love,

L

Dear Harriet,

Hillene's job involved dealing with customs and immigration. She had a sunny disposition, blonde hair, and blue eyes. The Sudanese men enjoyed having her joking around, and eventually completed her requests. On one occasion, immigration lost a passport, and no one seemed able to find it. Hillene asked if she could help them look for it, and they agreed. She looked through desk drawers and on the tops of desks. Then just by chance she looked under a desk, and there it was. Someone stuffed the passport under the leg of the desk to keep it from wobbling. Problem solved, she removed the passport and left the office workers to find another prop.

She took on the challenge of clearing a shipping container that arrived in Juba. Supplies of certain foods and other items were often difficult or impossible to get in the local market. So, we ordered a shipping container to be filled in the States and sent to us. The administration instructed the packers to put in personal items first, then the requested orders, and last, the food order.

Most items on the food order requested specific items and quantities. But in case space remained, they were to fill it with cake mixes, etc., in sufficient quantity to be divided among forty units.

I didn't want to miss the opportunity, so when I heard about the container, I asked my parents to prepare a box to put into the container. I made a list of the foods and goodies that I wanted, and Dad built a box of quarter-inch plywood to hold these things. Mom wrapped everything in at least one layer and sometimes more layers of plastic wrap. If I had been there, I would have scoffed at these precautions, but later I felt deeply grateful for them. The box was sent off to North Carolina to be included in the container shipment.

After leaving the U.S., for some unknown reason, it was off-loaded in Israel. After several months, it was located and put on another ship headed for Mombasa, Kenya. Once it was off-loaded in Mombasa, it had to clear customs and be transported by truck through Kenya and Uganda to Juba, a journey of 1,500 miles. That part of the trip was only supposed to take a week. Six weeks later, it turned up. The entire journey took eighteen months. The paperwork for the container needed to be cleared by customs before we opened it. However, we noted a large hole at the end of the container and rightly feared seawater had washed in.

Hillene began work on freeing the container. Every day, it was a new story of yet another piece of paper that had to be signed or another stamp that was needed. She carried around an enormous stack of papers from desk to desk. When she finished with one desk, she asked where to go next, and someone pointed to the next hurdle. One day, she arrived at the new desk to find no one there. The person working at that desk was supposed to stamp the papers, but he was out sick. "Where is his stamp?" she asked. The men rushed to find the stamp; they even broke open the locked drawer in which he kept it. She said, "Now stamp it!" No way. The only person who could do that was the man who sat at that desk and he was out sick, perhaps for several days.

Hillene, a resourceful person, then asked, "Where is his supervisor?" They pointed to the correct office and in she went. She explained her situation and asked if he would stamp her papers so she could continue with the process. No, he assured her, only that man could stamp her paper. Hmmm. Hillene realized he wouldn't do anything as long as those working in that office were standing around his desk. She asked if they could speak privately. The supervisor agreed. Once they were alone, she asked him again to stamp the papers, and he reluctantly refused. Ahh! She was making progress.

"What if I stamp the paper and you sign it? Would that make it okay?" she asked hopefully.

The supervisor thought for a few minutes, and his face brightened. "Yes," he replied, "that would be fine." So, she stamped the papers, and he signed them and she proceeded to the next desk.

For three weeks, things continued like this. One day, she asked where to go and the reply was, "You've finished. Go home."

"No, no, tell me where to go next!"

"No, there is nothing else. You can go home now." She was so excited she forgot to collect the keys to the locks on the container. After lunch, she had to track them down.

So, the great day had come—a year and a half after the container left the U.S. We were going to claim our things! There would be exciting food in the commissary and goodies from home. We would enter the computer age with our new desktops. We rallied around. The doors opened, and we saw the damage done by the seawater. Besides the leak, a few of the cans of soda had exploded. One soon-to-be-unpopular person had included a can of fiberglass resin in the shipment. It had broken open and leaked all over. The resulting mess was not a pleasant sight or odor. Under other circumstances, we would have thrown away most of it. But after all the waiting, we were determined nothing that remained salvageable would go to waste. At that point, I was thankful for the care my parents had taken in wrapping the items in my box. At least those items didn't smell like "container."

The food, which they should have loaded last, had gone in first and the extra goodies comprised ten cake mixes and small quantities of other things. We decided to just have a big party with those things and everyone who was present on the day could enjoy them since there were not enough to go around.

The computer had not fared so well. While it appeared to have dried out from all the liquids that had assaulted it, the inside was still damp. The director and his staff were eager to start playing with it, so they unpacked it and plugged it into the nearest electrical outlet, and blew it up. The entire circuit board and who knows what else had to be replaced. After replacements and repairs were completed, it served us well for many years.

Love,

L

———

Dear Harriet,

There was one aspect of the house we didn't control: the electricity. I had brought my solar system from the village but didn't have the skill needed to set it up. The wiring wasn't that complicated, but getting the solar panel attached to the roof required a tall ladder, a drill, and screws. Since the house was built of concrete blocks, it didn't lend itself to having nails hammered in the walls. There was metal sheeting on the roof. (And then there were the bats...) Without the solar panels, my battery soon ran down and we spent many hot, sticky nights with a kerosene lamp as our only source of light. Kirk, a colleague, came to our rescue. He had lived in a village east of Maridi in Western Equatoria with his family. Having that experience, he realized we might need a bit of help, so he volunteered to put up our solar system. We were deeply grateful! We had a solar light in each bedroom, the sitting room and the dining room/kitchen. Since Juba Power and Light was usually powerless and dark, it was nice to have a cooler source of light once more.

Sometimes we had electricity, and on those days, we enjoyed fans and fluorescent lights. One day, we were eating lunch and enjoying the fans turning around and cooling us off. The fuse box and electricity meter were on the wall near the dining room table. A light bulb attached to the fuse box lit up when the power came on. On that day, we noticed when the light bulb got brighter, the fans got very slow. A few seconds later, the light bulb dimmed, and the fans whizzed around with frightening speed. Back and forth, the lights and fans continued in cyclic opposition until at last, the light bulb was super bright and the fans stopped completely. We didn't know what to make of it. We looked at each other to make sure each of us saw it. Yes, this was happening.

We appealed to Tom, the electrical specialist amongst our col-leagues, to see what was going on. He arrived in the evening when the light was shining brightly on the "box" and the rest of the house was in total darkness. He held the light up to see if the numbers were moving on the meter, ironically using the light to see why we didn't have any light. It was a bizarre situation, and I decided we needed a photograph. I slipped into my room, got my camera, and snapped a picture. When the camera flashed, Tom jumped three feet in the air. He thought he had been electrocuted. When he came back to earth and his heart rate returned to normal, he checked the first juncture where the wires divided. When he touched the juncture, there was not enough power to get a spark—60 volts. The box had 320 volts. Clearly, there was a problem.

Tom returned the next day when the power was off. He removed the box from the wall and found that all the wires had melted together. It's a wonder the house hadn't burned down, except it's hard to burn concrete blocks. Most of the wiring in the house had to be replaced. While that was being done, another odd electrical event happened. Tom was testing the fluorescent lights. One of them flashed and flashed, but never stayed on. He took the starter out and the light came on. I turned off the switch, and the light went off. I turned on the switch and the light came on (without the starter). Then he put the starter in and the light went off. That isn't supposed to happen, but we both witnessed that it did. Electricity in Sudan is one of those things that remains a mystery.

Water was another challenge in the house. The water company installed pipes for many homes in Juba, but the pump that got the water to the homes malfunctioned or had no electricity. We lived for months without a single drop of water coming to our house from the city. The need for the water tank in our yard became more apparent. We stored water in 50-gallon drums, filled by a tanker truck that happened by infrequently or from rainwater that was caught by the house gutters. When those systems failed, the pilots brought three 50-gallon drums of water to our house on the back of a pickup. Then they used the pump for fueling the plane to get the water up into the tank. A little water remained at the bottom of the drums. This water was poured into buckets and basins for our neighbors, who sent their children over as soon as the truck drew up to the house. It was quite a sight to watch.

We got around 140 gallons of water once a week. If we ran out before the end of the week, we made do until someone had time to bring more. So, we strictly conserved our water use. We only flushed the toilet three times a day, took showers out of a bucket and a cup and tried to use as little water as possible for the cleaning and dishwashing. Our maid, Aurelia, never caught on that there was a water shortage. Countless times, I found her slowly washing the sink while letting the water run and watching it flow down the drain. Whenever I heard water running, I rushed out of my room shouting, "Turn off the water! Turn off the water!" She would glance at me, look at the water, look back at me, and slowly turn off the water (if I hadn't gotten there and turned it off myself). When she found another job, I was relieved.

Paul Otto, our next house helper previously mentioned in the ant story, was a blessing. He understood the problem with the water and conserved it like the precious liquid that it was. When he came to work for us, we offered to show him through the house. He was sixteen years old and in intermediate school. "Just give me a broom. I'll find my way." And he did. He observed our habits so well that by the second month, when Hillene came home from work, he asked, "One bucket or two?" He knew if she took a shower, she needed one bucket, but if she wanted to wash her hair, she needed two.

While Paul was working for us, we learned employees become part of the family. As family, employees expected they could ask for help when they needed something. One day, Paul came and asked us to help him. He needed some sheets and a sponge. The sheets we could understand, but a sponge? He was studying English in school and thought he had the correct vocabulary. But when we showed him a sponge that we used to clean, it was not the right thing. After further questioning, we understood that he wanted a foam mattress. He was sleeping on a grass mat on the ground. Now that he had regular employment, he wanted to upgrade. We helped him to get a loan to buy a metal bed as well. He used that bed until he got married. Then he gave it to his mother-in-law.

Paul has five daughters and a son now, and, as I expected, he proved himself to be an excellent manager and remains a good friend.

Love,

L

Dear Harriet,

Most of the windows of our house opened straight onto someone else's courtyard, which gave us an excellent view of our neighbor's lives. They also caught glimpses of our life. The back windows were up high, so they didn't afford a view into our bedrooms or bathroom. It was easy to watch people's movements behind us because there were no fences. One day, I was sitting at my desk working on my analysis of Shilluk when I overheard shouting. It paid to be alert to one's environment, and I decided I better find out what the shouting and carrying on was about. I didn't understand the words, but the actions became clear without them.

The neighbors called a man from his work to return home. When he arrived, the neighbors explained a snake had crawled into his one-room hut. They saw it go in but didn't see it leave. It impressed me that his neighbors had seen the snake and then sent someone to get the man. Neighbors looked after one another. Many Africans assume every snake is poisonous. If you aren't sure, that is the best way to approach the issue of a snake hiding in your house. Someone lent the man a spear. He carefully checked the grass roof at the entrance, then unlocked the door and threw it open. It was dark inside, as the small windows didn't let in much light.

He peered into the dark room for a few minutes, letting his eyes adjust. I stood transfixed at my window, wondering what he would do next. Then I wondered if I might call on him to find a snake in my house if one ever crawled in! He said he would have to go inside after studying the room as far as he could. The neighbors stood at a safe distance, scanning the outside of the hut in case the snake crawled out. The man kept asking if they had seen it yet, to which they answered, "No, not yet."

Reluctantly, he entered the room, and I imagined him studying the beams in the ceiling and the grass in the roof. I heard him moving the furniture. We waited for what felt like a lifetime. Suddenly, he began shouting and knocking things over. At last, he emerged carrying the four-foot-long, light green serpent skewered on the spear. He took it down the street to the oohs and ahs of neighbors. I thought back to my snake lectures at the orientation course and wondered if it was a green mamba!

Love,

L

Dear Harriet,

Martin, Helga, and their boys lived in Eastern Equatoria among a group called the Toposa. They had spent years in a cluster of settlements called Riwoto learning the Toposa language and culture.

Eastern Equatoria was one of the last places to be controlled by the British when they helped Egypt rule Sudan. The Toposa are tall and thin. The men think of clothing more as a decorative item than a necessity. They raise cattle for a living and believe that when God created the world, he gave all the cattle to the Toposa. If the neighboring tribes had cattle, they assumed the owners had stolen them. They had to reclaim their animals. Since that belief is common among the various ethnic groups in the region, they regularly stole cattle from each other.

Martin and Helga received an invitation to a wedding for a local man. The groom's family invited everyone to attend the festivities. The groom was generally older, as he would have enough oxen to pay the bride price. The bride was normally young. The occasion that Martin and Helga attended the *nyakuuma* ceremony that completed the marriage process. The groom and his family were expected to pay paid up to 100 oxen, cows, and bulls to the bride's family. Since the bride was going to his family, she represented a certain amount of work. Her parents had to be compensated for the loss of that labor. The representatives of the families met in a hut for the talks and bargaining went on most of the night.

Everyone else got to dance. The drums beat their throbbing rhythms and men performed war dance moves and shouted praises to their favorite bull. Food was served, and the women sang and clapped. At intervals, the groom-to-be, overcome with excitement, rushed out of the hut and began leaping and whirling about, fully clothed only in a suit jacket. Yes, I mean the only thing he wore was the jacket.

The bride typically sat, looking very sad. Sometimes that was genuinely how she felt, as she might be in love with one of the young warriors. Perhaps she didn't want to marry the older man to whom she was being engaged. Even if she was happy, she had to look sad. That evening, the groom took her to his village and she became the youngest wife of her husband's household. Her lot would not be an easy one, so weddings often were not festive occasions for the female half of the union.

Love,

L

———

Dear Harriet,

As Christmas 1983 approached, I felt sad as I looked over the events of the year since I left Khartoum. My language-learning days seemed long ago and far away, and the intervening year was full of stress and uncertainty. Every day brought more news that angered the southerners. The central government began implementing Islamic law, so there were riots at the university and men getting drunk to defy the Islamic ban on drinking alcohol. The Sudan People's Liberation Movement (SPLM) continued to gain strength and rumors abounded that they planned to attack Juba. When there was no news, hope grew that the situation might settle down and calm might be restored. Then the news reports started again. The insecurity pushed me to work harder since I did not know how long I could stay in Sudan.

To lighten the mood, our household tried to join in various activities celebrating the Christmas season. Sister Theresa told us about a Christmas carol competition sponsored by the churches. We went along to enjoy the music.

Two or three songs were prepared by the church choirs. As they announced each group, the choir began a slow and practiced procession toward the outdoor stage, singing their first song. I say "slow and practiced" because they choreographed the movements in different ways, either a shuffle step or three steps forward and two steps back, all synchronized. Each group took three to five minutes to get to the stage, but they had greeted us in song by the time they arrived. The songs varied greatly as well. Some songs were in their local language and style of music, using traditional instruments. Others used Western songs sung in either English or Arabic, but with a Sudanese flavor to the music. While Western music has an eight-note scale, most Sudanese music has a five-note scale. Thus, many of the half tones (sharps and flats) were not there, giving a distinct quality to the music.

One group used a marimba made with two sheaves of grass under different-sized wooden blocks. The musician tapped the blocks with sticks and produced a lovely sound. Another group brought lyres that I had never seen before. The base looked similar to a boat with the bow cut off, while the prow was long and curved. Strings stretched from the prow along the top of the "boat." They covered the body of the instrument with the skin of an animal. Eight people each played a small lyre, plucking it as they sang. Four others carried in one large lyre, and it took all of them to lift it. One person played it to add a lovely, deep tone. A choir sang with this interesting accompaniment. Sister Theresa told me that in Shilluk this instrument is called an *aduung*. The group, however, had brought it from Uganda.

The clothing choices of a few of the participants provided another source of entertainment. For an occasion of this significance, everyone had dressed up in their finest. The women wore dresses or skirts and blouses; the men wore trousers and shirts. A couple of people broke the mold. One man appeared wearing a pair of baby's rubber underpants on his head for a hat. Another young woman wore a short see-through nightie. She wore a bra under it, so it was not so revealing. Seeing an outfit like that in public remains unique in my experience.

I don't know which choir won, and it didn't matter. Thankfully, this occasion lifted our spirits and prepared us for the coming celebration.

Love,

L

———

Dear Harriet,

One morning as I was trying to work out the English equivalent of a complicated Shilluk text, I heard wailing coming from a neighbor's house. I peeped out of the back window and saw family members arriving, wailing as they came. Someone in the house had died. We didn't know the family and did not know what to do in this situation, so we watched out the window and asked questions of our friends.

The *bika* or wake lasted for three days. During that time, hundreds of people turned up. This was the flip side of going to an office and finding the person you most needed to see had "gone to the funeral of a relative." All the relatives had turned up. Of course, families were not immediate family as we think of it, but extended family. So, every one of the fourth cousins twice removed turned up, as well as brothers, sisters, father, mother, sons and daughters, and their families. Of course, friends must go. Since relationships and friendships were diligently cultivated, it was imperative to turn up to express their grief and sit for a while with the family. In Shilluk culture, if you don't go to the funeral, they may assume you were responsible for the person's death.

The men came quietly; not the women. I watched more than one woman walk along the road chatting to her friends until she got twenty yards from the house. At that point, she burst out into loud cries of anguish and grief, throwing herself on the ground as if in her own death throes. Family members came to assist her to a chair or a mat on the ground. Her crying continued as long as appropriate to express sadness at this loss. Then the tears turned off as she chatted with friends or family. When another mourner turned up, everyone cried again. I don't mean to imply there was not genuine grief. But if the deceased was not a close friend or relative, it was polite to wail as if he or she were dearly loved, at least for a while.

Once seated, one of the many girls pressed into service brought a glass of water on a small tray. These girls may have been family members or neighbors' daughters who came along to help. We discovered that the husband in our neighbor's house had died and the widow was grieving and possibly in a state of shock. I don't know how many children they had, but most of our neighbors appeared to be young. I guessed there were small children in the household. The mourning lasted for three days, showing it was the man who died. Had it been the wife who died, the mourning would have taken five days. The time of mourning and customs that were followed differed with each language group. This household was Bari, one of the larger ethnic groups in Equatoria.

Many mourners came from a distance, so they stayed at the house. The household where the death occurred was expected to provide food for all visitors. That seemed an impossible require-ment, given the poverty of most people. It must have taken years to pay off a funeral. When I attended a wake, there was a basket discreetly placed where people put in contributions to help the family. I hope that was the case for our neighbor.

The actual burial took place at once since the climate was hot and there was no reliable refrigeration. I learned in Bari culture, if a wife died and her husband had not yet completed paying the dowry for her, they could not bury her until they made full payment. Now THAT is called "incentive!"

The other inescapable part of this funeral was the drumming. They played a large drum at various intervals during the day and the night. They sang mourning songs and danced in a special style used for funerals. We were glad when they got tired and stopped sometime after midnight, so we could get to sleep.

A few weeks later, I was at the office when one of our employees, Pasquale, came to ask if someone would drive one of the group vehicles to help with a burial. I volunteered. Before I could ask questions, we were in the Toyota pickup. When we came to a compound, Pasquale told me to stop and wait. He got out of the truck and entered the house. A few minutes later, a woman appeared and got in the front seat beside me, holding a baby wrapped in a blanket. Pasquale joined us while several men piled into the back. I was waiting for the body, but Pasquale told me to go ahead. It was then that I realized it was the baby in the mother's arms who had died. My heart went out to her, but she had no tears and showed no emotion. She sat there quietly as we bounced slowly through the dirt streets of Juba.

Back on to the tarmac road, Pasquale directed me toward army headquarters. Instead of driving onto the army base, we took off through the grass to a cemetery. Someone had dug a grave, so as we drew up, the men jumped down. Pasquale helped the woman out of the cab, still holding her dead child. I shut off the engine, got out, and followed the procession to the graveside. I did not know what to expect but felt sad for this poor young woman. There was no service. I had assumed there would be. No priest or pastor attended, no talking at all. There was just silence as they placed the child in the blanket in the grave and covered the little body with earth. The mother was silent; she shed not one tear. When the burial was completed, people began walking back toward the truck.

At that point, the talking started, and it was not quiet! The men shouted at each other and the woman joined in. Not knowing the language, I was mystified. I sat in the truck, wondering what to do next. After half an hour, the shouting and arguing attracted the army and soldiers came to investigate. I learned that the husband's family failed to make the proper payments after the child's birth and the wife's family was threatening to take their daughter back. The soldiers insisted they finish their argument at home and not near the base. Everyone got back into the pickup, and Pasquale instructed me to return them to town. I didn't ask questions, just headed back. They got out near their compound and I returned the pickup to the center, still mystified at what I had seen.

Later I asked Pasquale why the mother hadn't cried. He explained they believed if a mother gives birth and the child dies soon after, the child's soul waits around for some time. If the mother cries, showing that she misses the child, the soul of that child will enter the body of the next child she conceives. They believe that child will also die. So, everyone had to pretend not to care about the death so the next child she has may live. What a lot to ask of a mother!

Love,

L

———

Dear Harriet,

The day after Christmas, I was back at work again typing up lists of Shilluk words. Personal computers hadn't yet come to my part of the world, so I was using a typewriter. (The two desktop computers from the container were for the administration's use.) As I sat at my desk, I noticed the sound of drumming. My first thought was, *Oh no, not another funeral!* But it wasn't that type of drumming. Looking out my back window, I saw four men standing on the road with a large drum. They were talking and laughing and periodically beating on the drum. They were still celebrating the season, and it looked like a great photo opportunity. I slipped over to the cupboard where I kept my camera, opened it, checked the settings, put it up against the screen, aimed and, *click*, took the photo. At the sound of the click, the men looked up at my window. They saw me and shouted something. I disappeared from view.

Within minutes, Cathy and I heard shouting outside our gate and a crowd of men pushed open our unlocked door to the street. Cathy had been washing clothes in the yard, as our regular house help was off for the holidays. She gave a little cry as about fifty men entered our compound. I hurried out of the house and confessed that I had taken a picture without permission. I thought she was going to kill me. But there was no time for that, as the men began playing the drum, dancing, and singing.

The neighbors came for a look, crowding into our small yard to watch the free entertainment. The leader of the dancers indicated I could take pictures, so I got out my camera and took a few shots. I even got out the cassette recorder and recorded the singing and drumming. The dancing involved holding their arms in different positions over their heads and jumping up and down. The arm movements represented the various shapes of the horns of the cow. I'm not sure what the jumping symbolized, but they could jump pretty high, though I expect they could have jumped higher if they hadn't been quite so drunk.

One neighbor who spoke some English explained that the dancers were Dinka celebrating Christmas. I asked my neighbor what I should do to get rid of them. He said, "Pay them something."

"How much?"

"Whatever you have." Cathy and I had the Sudanese equivalent of $5 in small bills, so we counted that out. The leader approved the amount, led one more dance, and then they all departed to have a few more drinks. The neighbors followed them, having enjoyed the show.

As we locked the gate behind the last person, Cathy and I looked at each other and breathed a sigh of relief. Then she told me I was NEVER to take another photograph out of my window without her express permission!

Love,

L

Dear Harriet,

As time passed, the tensions in Juba increased. The Sudan People's Liberation Army (SPLA) had replaced the former Anya Nya and were reportedly moving closer to Juba each week. They ran their own radio station, and Sister Theresa was a regular listener. We faithfully listened to Focus on Africa from the BBC. The garrison in Juba was a predictable target for an attack. The SIL-Sudan policy said if we felt unsafe, we were free to leave. No one wanted to look like a weakling, so many stayed. We always wondered if the stories were true, and how were we to know if the rebels were really THAT close?

Two young Irishmen, who visited our house now and then, spent a week at the Catholic seminary compound on the Kit River, near Juba. One evening, after everyone had gone to bed, a contingent of SPLA soldiers arrived. They entered the dorm and took any valuables and clothes that they could find. One room contained a locked medicine cabinet. They asked who kept the key. The seminarians pointed to a young man who was "sleeping" soundly on his bed. The soldiers did everything they could to wake this boy, but he "slept" through it all. They even picked him up and put him on the floor to search his bed for the key. The boy didn't wake up, and they couldn't find the key. Ultimately, the soldiers left.

The next morning, the priest sent the Irishmen back to Juba wearing clothes that had been in the laundry. After returning to their unit with the goods, the soldiers mentioned there were two Irish boys in the compound. The officer in charge ordered them to return to the compound and bring the Irishmen back. By the time the soldiers arrived, the boys were long gone. From this report, we realized just how close the SPLA were.

A few weeks later, the priest came into Juba to withdraw money from the bank. He put it in his briefcase. This priest's nickname was

Father Christmas because of his long white beard. Father Christmas stopped off at the Catholic compound in Juba for a visit before returning home. During this visit, he set down his briefcase with the money in the hallway. When he left, he forgot to pick up the briefcase, and returned home without it.

That night, the SPLA paid him another visit. This time, they entered his house and demanded that he hand over all his money. He showed them he had almost no money, as it was sitting in the hallway in Juba. His poor memory served him well!

When the SPLA realized this, they decided to take the priest as their hostage. They ordered him to go with them, threatening him with their guns. However, the priest had been around Sudan for a long time and knew the nature of the Sudanese. He told them he was very busy and did not have time to go with them. He said this firmly and repeatedly. In the end, they said, "Okay" and left.

I don't know what the commanding officer made of that, but Father Christmas moved himself and his seminary into Juba and stayed there. He didn't want to take the chance that he would escape so easily next time. With these events, we recognized where the lines were drawn.

Love,

L

———————

Dear Harriet,

After our eventful Christmas, New Year's Eve passed peacefully. Hillene was away and Cathy and I started planning each other's lives, as people do at the end of a year. She expected to get her Ph.D., and during the evening, she decided I should get one as well.

Here we sat on December 31, 1983, deciding that I should go to England and study. I couldn't have been less skeptical if you had told me I was going to land on the moon in five years. I laughed and told her she was crazy and our conversation moved on to other things.

That night when in bed, the thought flitted through my head once more, and again, I dismissed it as nonsense. Two degrees and further graduate work in linguistics had convinced me I never wanted to take another examination. I was an intelligent human being. Why should I have to prove anything to anyone again? No, that was not for me. Then I heard "that voice" inside my head saying, *Don't say you can't get a Ph.D. That is what I want you to do.*

Yikes! I'm supposed to do what?

I researched several options and discovered that in England, you can read for a Ph.D. There are no exams except the final oral examination on the work you complete. I could take classes as long as they were useful and then stop when they weren't. It was totally up to me. I requested an application to the University of London, School of Oriental and African Studies.

My life would never be the same again.

Love,

L

―――――――――

Dear Harriet,

Seasons in the south differed from in the north. In the 1,000 miles between Khartoum and Juba, the climate shifted, and we were still 600 miles above the equator. While in Khartoum, when we had lovely winter weather, Juba was hot! When Khartoum was hot, Juba had rain. It rained from April through November, with the last rain on, or around, Christmas. The atmosphere got muggy and hot, and the clouds got heavier each day. Then the heavens opened as if someone had tipped over a huge bucket. It was less like drops of water and more like standing under a waterfall. After my year in Khartoum with little rain, I was fascinated by the water pouring down and then running through the streets. Thankfully, soil in Juba absorbed the water and there were enough hills that it ran off and didn't stand in large lakes as it had in Khartoum.

Our metal roof had advantages and disadvantages. It was hot when the sun shone and loud when it was raining. But it caught an abundance of water. Just a few feet of guttering in a strategic place where several angles of the roof came together, and it filled a fifty-gallon drum in twenty minutes! But we couldn't afford the luxury of just sitting around watching a drum fill. If someone were home, as I normally was, Paul and I grabbed buckets and dipped water from the outside barrel to fill up the inside barrels. We kept three barrels in the pantry. It rained so hard that with both of us removing several gallons of water every minute or two, the outside barrel still overflowed. When every available container in the house was full, we stood at the window to watch.

Our neighbors didn't have metal roofs. You can't catch water off a grass roof. When the rains came, and the ground was muddy, it was a good time for everyone to do house repairs or put up a new building in their compound. They dug holes approximately three feet in diameter. The holes filled up when it rained, but they also filled up with groundwater for days after the rain. The neighbors had put a fresh coat of mud mixed with cow dung or donkey dung on the house. After that, the groundwater saved them trips to the Nile or a local water pump. The pond provided water for washing dishes and bathing. By the way, the dung mixed with the mud serves as an excellent insect repellent, especially for termites. It also makes the house more waterproof.

With the excessive amounts of water that came off our back roof, the land behind our house became waterlogged. Neighbors dug a big hole back there! There was plenty of water available in the hole during August and September and even into October. The ten- to twelve-year-old girls from the neighborhood's many families often stood around waiting to fill their buckets or five-gallon jerry cans or plastic containers. By November, the water began drying up, and it took longer for the hole to fill. The younger girls came with smaller containers and a cup. Each one dipped the water out with the cup and filled her container, put it on her head and returned home. The hole was just outside my bedroom window, so I got a good look at the process.

By January 1984, very little water remained in the hole and the five- and six-year-olds arrived with tiny containers. Each after-noon, as I lay down for my nap, I heard a cup scraping on the bottom of that hole, trying to get any drop of water. The little girls laughed, teased each other and, as I have related elsewhere, bounced balls against my screen window, hoping to catch sight of the foreigner. It was too dry for them to bother anymore by the end of January, and the hole was abandoned until the next rainy season.

One other feature that came with the rain was thievery. The rain made so much noise on the metal roof that we failed to hear a man jump over the wall and siphon fuel out of the car. No one ever tried to get in the house. But no matter what precautions we took, if we had a long rainstorm during the night, there would be no fuel in the morning. Other than that, we were glad to see the rain.

Love,

L

Dear Harriet,

Mom and Dad came for a visit to Kenya, and I flew from Juba to meet them and act as tour guide. We had a lovely time together, and it was something we will never forget. One part of the visit was a real "African experience."

Before I left for Africa in 1982, I met two Kenyan families in the U.S. We got to be friends, and they, of course, had relatives back in Nairobi. While in Nairobi, I linked up with them. They were Kikuyu, the largest language group in Kenya. Joram offered to take Mom, Dad, and me out to visit a Maasai home.

On the appointed day, Joram, his wife, and two of the smaller children picked us up in his *matatu*. A *matatu* is a small pickup truck with a roof on the back and is used for public transport. We headed off toward the south into Maasai land. Joram had a Kikuyu friend who taught school there. The local chief, who was blind, invited us to lunch. Even with this handicap, he had enough resources to marry a second wife. We spent the day with this man and the bride-to-be. She looked about seventeen years old, while the groom-to-be was in his fifties. As in south Sudan, older men are the ones with enough cattle to pay bride prices. Men with several wives and lots of children have high status.

Our lunch was in the back room of the local shop. Dad checked out the supplies in the shop and found only a few cans of tomato sauce, some boxes of matches, and a bit of flour. I had cautioned my parents before this outing that when they served us a meal, we should not ask what it was, but receive it with thanks and eat it. When the time came for lunch, it was meat and potato stew, so nothing weird to choke down. They piled our bowls high, with far more than we would eat. Following our Kikuyu friend's lead, Mother and I asked to have some of the food returned to the pot as we could not eat all of it! This was acceptable. I looked over at Dad and realized that he was not eating. I asked if everything was all right. He said, "No, I can't eat this!"

"Why not?"

"These people are so poor; how can I eat their food?" I explained once again that it would be an insult not to eat it and that, as honored guests, he had to. So, somehow, he managed.

As a gesture of thanks for this hospitality, Joram had brought fruit to give to our host. The Maasai eat milk and meat, and fruit is never on the menu. The chief had never eaten an orange, and the ones we brought were sour. He tasted it and then asked why we ate them.

After the meal, we went to look at the house. It was low and round and made of mud. The women built the homes, and we had to double over to go inside. It was dark and smoky since they cooked in the middle of the structure. As we walked through the house, it felt like walking through a shell with concentric circles leading ever inward. The fireplace was in the very center. A hole in the roof drew the smoke out. But some of the smoke stayed in and damaged people's eyes. It felt good to get outside and stand upright again.

There weren't any cows, because the drought had forced the cattle to move closer to a water source. We noted the huge thorn fences that surrounded the compound and formed an enclosure for the cattle. Those thorn fences prevented predators from attacking the people and the animals. The Maasai are known as fierce warriors, and the test of manhood is to kill a lion using only a spear. We were most interested in killing flies. They were everywhere. We could barely talk without one flying into our mouths. The dung from the cattle seemed to cause the fly infestation. So, we were not too sorry to bid our host farewell and start back home.

On the way, a man was thumbing for a lift. We were in the middle of nowhere, so we were likely the only car he had seen for some time. Joram stopped to explain that there was no room in the vehicle, but the man seized the opportunity and jumped in the back. Mom and Dad were in the front with Joram, while Joram's wife, children, and I sat in the back. This guy just joined us. Always room for one more in Africa!

Hours later, in Nairobi, Joram turned to take us back to the guesthouse. Mom and Dad reminded him of the passenger in the back. He pulled over and went to ask the man where he wanted to be dropped off. He wanted to ride farther into town with them. As we got out of the *matatu* and said our farewells, this guy joined in as if he were part of the family. He got his picture taken and even asked for the camera. They left, and we collapsed on our beds for the night.

The next day, as we returned from an outing, we saw the hitch-hiker walking up to us. I don't know how he got on the compound. He asked if he could talk to Mom. This sounded suspicious, so I stayed close by. He asked if she would do him a favor when she returned to America. "What kind of favor?"

"Would you send me a truck?"

"A what!?" Mom asked incredulously.

"A truck, a pickup truck," he stated as boldly as that.

Mom was speechless with amazement. I intervened and explained several reasons why this was not going to happen and sent him on his way. It still amazes Mom anyone could make such a request of a virtual stranger. It was her introduction to the philosophy, "If you don't ask, you don't get."

Love,

L

———————

Dear Harriet,

Back in Juba, I visited our neighbors, who were boiling water for tea. They used charcoal as fuel in a square metal *kanoon* (burner). I suspect they make them from used tin cans. The burner was approximately twelve inches square with two layers. The top layer had one-inch strips of metal interlaced like a woven potholder. They placed the charcoal on the top metal layer for short tasks. She placed a thin aluminum pot on the coals. They put the charcoal in the bottom part if something needed to cook longer.

My neighbor told me the Arabic word for "ants" as she removed the pot filled with boiling water from the coals with her bare hands. *OUCH!* I thought. *That must hurt.* Then she moved the live coals around so they lay more evenly, again with her bare hands. Afterwards, she replaced the pot onto the coals. Even though it was hot, she wasn't in a hurry to put down the pot.

"Doesn't that hurt your hands?"

"Yes," she replied.

"Why don't you use a cloth or something?"

She shrugged as if it were easier to just use her hands. I have seen this same practice in many homes and can confirm they have a high tolerance for touching hot things.

But we found their weak spot! The little boys in the neighborhood liked to open the gate for us when we drove home. Then they asked their usual question: "Do you have any tins?" They collected tin cans to make toy cars. One day I had defrosted the freezer, and the sink was full of ice. As I handed out the tins, I asked if they had ever seen ice. Few homes had electricity, so the locals rarely had anything to do with ice. The boys said they hadn't ever seen any. I said we had some, and they wanted to find out what it was like. I carried the ice out in my hand and gave each of them a little to hold. They tossed the ice back and forth from hand to hand, shrieking and howling. It hurt them! I guess we get used to holding cold things, and they get used to holding hot things. If the holding doesn't last too long, it doesn't hurt either of us.

Sister Theresa went to India for church meetings. She traveled through Nairobi to reach India and returned by the same route. Soon after she got back, I asked her opinion of India. It horrified her that people lived in such abject poverty and could not work to change their status. The caste system was anathema to her. Even though many of the people living in Juba were just as poor, the freedom to work and provide for their families made it bearable. One comment remains with me. She said, "They are poorer than the poorest wood cutter in the village, but they are not happy."

I asked if it was cold in Nairobi. She assured me it was very cold in Nairobi. In fact, "it was as cold as fire!" I've reflected on that comparison, and have concluded that sometimes the cold burns, like fire.

Love,

L

Dear Harriet,

I mentioned last time the children liked tin cans, but initially I was confused as to what they wanted. They asked for *taskar* and the only Arabic word I knew was *taskara*, "a ticket." So, I asked where they wanted to go. I was thinking of a plane ticket or a bus ticket. Finally, I realized they were asking for Tusker, which was a brand of local beer that came in a tin can. It was not surprising they thought I had lost my mind.

Once that got sorted out, I explained we didn't drink beer, so we didn't have any Tusker cans. They asked if we had other tins, which we did. They became the recyclers for our tin cans. We put the empty tins on the screened porch. When they asked, we looked at the screen porch to see what was available. They rarely left disappointed.

We insisted they learn to ask politely. Some days, ten little boys ranging in age from five to twelve surrounded us, and it felt more like a mugging. So, we gradually taught them to greet us, according to the time of day. Then they opened the car door and helped get our things into the house. Once we locked the car door, they could ask, *"Eilba fii?"* ("Are there any tins?") Once they had their tins, they learned to say "Thank you," and off they went, closing the gate behind them.

On the whole, we had good relations with the neighbors. Tensions continued to increase with news of approaching rebels. The administration instructed us on various emergency procedures. We kept enough food and water in the house to last for several days. But the problem I faced was knowing when the emergency started. We had no phones, and we often walked back and forth to the SIL compound. As a household, we talked about strategies in case we were on the street when something bad happened. We agreed we would not hesitate to enter any compound along the way to ask for refuge. It was certain that it would be offered.

Love,

L

Dear Harriet,

You may wonder what the boys did with those tin cans. They might have used them to store things or sold them in the market. But the most creative use was to make toys. These families had very little, and keeping children fed was a top priority. The next priority was a roof over their heads, and then came school fees. Children are the same the world over. They like to play. Since they could not afford the few toys available in the market, they made their own.

They used sharp stones or possibly their mother's kitchen knives and who knows what else to beat the cans into flat sheets and cut the sheets into the desired shapes. And yes, the edges were VERY sharp. They fastened the pieces together with small bits of wire and created a Suzuki Jeep, Land Rover, fighter jet, or Toyota pickup truck. If they saw it, they copied it.

They made each car tire of a circle of old flip-flops, attached to the axle by bits of the flip-flop strap. A nail or sturdy piece of wire served as the axle, with a bottle cap as the hubcap. A small bit of inner tube served as mud flaps on the back wheels. The bumpers, grille, everything matched the real thing! The shiny metal was outside, but on the underside, it was easy to distinguish the Raid cans from the oatmeal or the milk tins. They wasted nothing. Cars made by the smaller children just had the outside shell, but the older children re-created the inside seats, steering wheel and even the engine. I bought one car that flashed the lights if I put a battery in the small compartment on its underside.

I don't know how many fingers they lost or how many contracted tetanus from this hazardous occupation. The children tied a string to the front bumper and pulled the cars along, bouncing along the dusty path just the way the real ones bounced over the dirt roads. The suspension was even the same. When riding in my Suzuki Jeep over the rough roads, I often thought of how similar it was to the toys the children made.

I didn't see too many girls playing. Girls helped their mothers with minor tasks from the time they were able to walk. It was common to see a three- or four-year-old girl carrying her baby sister or brother. They sent girls of five or six with a little money to buy a soda for a visitor from the neighborhood shop. They helped with washing the dishes and their own clothes. Fetching water was another time-consuming task for young girls. I watched with envy as a five-year-old filled her water container from the hole outside my window, perched the two-pint container on her head, and gracefully walked down the road. If I had started at that age, perhaps I could walk along with something balanced on my head. Women filled large five-gallon plastic oil jugs with water, and other women had to help lift the heavy jug up onto her head. But once it was there, she balanced it with one hand and carried it home.

Girls in a family learned to clean, cook, do chores, and care for their brothers and father. As they got older, they took on most of the household tasks. Mothers then had time to crochet, knit, gossip with the neighbors, or just supervise. After growing up without time to play, women could enjoy some leisure time. The matron of the household preferred to sit in her chair and watch the rest of the household doing the work. Her family bought food, prepared and served it, and then cleared up. They cleaned the house and washed and ironed clothes. Guests were served and welcomed without her having to move from her "throne." Since they worked through their early years, I guess they deserved it. It was also a clear sign that she managed a successful household.

Of course, without daughters in the home, things didn't run as smoothly. When she needed help, she found a reason to visit a relative who had several girls in the house and borrowed one. One woman I knew had taken in several girls to help with the housework after her own daughters grew up and married. These relatives attended school as compensation for their services. Girls often get little education because they need to work in the house or fields. The prevailing thought is, "How does schooling help a girl do her housework better?"

On the topic of education, during this time I sent off my one-page application and received an acceptance letter to "read for an M. Phil degree." In England, they don't just let you into a Ph.D. program. One has to prove one's ability for research and writing. So, the M. Phil is a Master of Philosophy, and if that's all you get, it indicates you failed the Ph.D. requirements. It was a start, though, and in September 1984, I made my way to London to begin my studies.

Love,

L

Dear Harriet,

As I stood in the queue for British immigration, I suddenly thought, *Where are those papers I prepared to show authorities here?* I had asked Wycliffe UK to sponsor me while I was in England, and they had produced the required letter. I also had the letter from SOAS, inviting me to study. But I was under a great deal of stress when I left Juba, and now I couldn't remember what I had done with those important pieces of paper.

As the queue inched forward, I decided to behave as a good Sudanese would in such a situation. Upon arrival at the desk of the immigration officer, I greeted him with joy and lightness in my voice. He replied in kind. I handed him my passport and he asked, "How long are you going to stay in the U.K.?"

"Oh, about a year."

"And what are you going to do here?" he inquired.

"I've been offered a place at the University of London, School of Oriental and African Studies to read for a Ph.D."

"Very good," he responded. "Do you have a letter about that?"

"Yes," I replied confidently.

"Could I see it?"

"No."

"And why not?" he asked.

"I left it in my luggage," I said with a look of chagrin.

"How are you going to pay for this?"

"The organization I work for is sponsoring me," I replied confidently.

"Do you have a letter about that?"

"Yes," I answered.

"Can I see it?" he asked. By this time, he was not looking as welcoming.

"No," I admitted.

"Why not?"

"I left it in my luggage," came my apologetic answer. "Would you like me to go get my luggage?"

"Yes." He held on to my passport as I went to retrieve my suitcases.

Do you know that feeling that you can't remember what's in your luggage until it finally appears, and you know what you want isn't in there? When my suitcases appeared—and they were last off the plane—I knew the letters weren't there. I felt a rising panic as I started searching through the endless random papers in my hand-carry. It took so long that the immigration officer came looking for me. He could see the fear and frustration on my face.

He said, "I'll let you in this time, but next time do NOT put your papers in your luggage!"

I assured him I would never make that mistake again, and he stamped a visa into my passport. There is no doubt In my mind that today, such a thing would never happen. But the world was a different place in 1984.

The papers turned up. One was actually in the hand carry that came with me; I discovered it after unpacking. The other letter was in my air freight that didn't arrive for several weeks. No immigration official ever asked to see them again.

Love,

L

Chapter 7

A Research Year in Juba

Dear Harriet,

When seeking to earn a doctorate degree in England, it is called "reading for a Ph.D.," and that is exactly what you do. The library at the School of Oriental and African Studies (SOAS) has one of the best collections of books related to African languages. I discovered books in Shilluk I had never seen in Sudan. The numerous linguistic and African journals were up to date. There was no lack of things to read.

I spent a year reading about linguistics, attending classes, and getting acquainted with Shilluks, Ethiopians, Ghanaians, and Nigerians. I related more easily to the Africans than the British. It was good to be out of the stress, heat, and pressure, but my heart was still in Africa. So, when my tutor suggested I spend a year back in Sudan to collect more information, I eagerly agreed.

In October 1985, I found myself once again in Juba, taking a study leave from my coursework to clarify the many issues in Shilluk that were boggling my mind. I'd learned enough to understand what I couldn't explain. Perhaps the point of education is to discover how little we know. It is a topic for another time.

I arrived on a Monday, and Hillene collected me from the airport. The weather was HOT. That evening, Sister Theresa joined us single folks for dinner at the Greek Club. It was fun to catch up with old friends.

On Tuesday, I moved into a one-bedroom apartment at the center, but by Saturday, my head was in a daze and I slept more than usual. The effort of arriving and adjusting to the heat and humidity had taken its toll, and I felt quite fragile and tired. About 2:00, someone knocked on my door and I staggered over to see who it was.

The news that bandits had shot the sister-in-law of my colleague, Jon, jolted me into wakefulness. She and her husband were driving on a road in Eastern Equatoria when bandits started shooting at their car. Her husband quickly drove away from the bandits, even though bullets punctured the tires. The bullet that did the most damage had gone through the door and the seat and into Janice. He drove as quickly as he could to the nearest airstrip and radioed Juba for help. They diverted a plane preparing to take off from Juba airport to collect Janice and her husband. They returned to Juba and doctors tried to stabilize her condition before flying on to Nairobi for treatment. She lay under the wing of the plane as people came to give blood and offer encouragement to her husband. After some hours, the couple took off for Nairobi, but she died on the way. The challenges of life in Sudan had not eased, nor had the tension decreased while I was away.

Love,

L

Dear Harriet,

Over the course of the next week, I worked on my data and got reacquainted with various friends. My routine included regular trips to the USAID pool. Yes, things were settling down and by

Thursday, I saw some progress. I was reading in my apartment in the evening, enjoying the fact that Juba's power was on for the first time since I arrived. Suddenly, the power went off, and I heard gunshots. There were red flashes through the sky, clearly visible in the darkness. I hurried outside to see what was going on. That was the wrong thing to do, but by the time I realized it, I was already outside. I learned later that one family hid under the bed for most of the evening, as they didn't know what it meant either. It turned out not to be an attack by the SPLA. However, explanations varied from "the army shooting tracer bullets over town to practice" to "a celebration that the government had taken the town of Bor from the SPLA," which had been announced over the Juba radio in Arabic earlier in the day. But I, along with most of my colleagues, had not heard the announcement, so this had come as a complete surprise to us.

Another regular feature of life was fighter jets screeching through the skies over Juba. Southerners often looked up and shook their fists at the planes before the jets flew off on a bombing mission. Despite this distraction, I re-engaged my mind to work by the following Friday. A band was playing, and we heard shouting as the army celebrated (or prepared to celebrate) the retaking of the town of Bor. A plane zoomed about more than usual. I didn't think too much about it until my colleague, Anne, arrived at the center in quite an emotional state. She had seen the jet crash in the middle of town, near her house. She had watched in horror as it fell to the ground.

We learned the plane had been practicing aerial stunts for the celebration when it developed engine trouble. One version of the story claimed the mechanics told the pilot to take the plane up for a trial run to see if they had fixed the problem. When the engine failed, the pilot tried to ditch the plane in the Nile, but he didn't make it that far. As he flew over the main market, burning fuel fell on people, injuring many of them. The plane crashed in a square near the center of town. Our director investigated and found a hole at least six feet deep where the plane had crashed. There wasn't a piece of the plane bigger than a square foot. The debris was strewn for half a mile. The pilot didn't survive. Juba was not a peaceful place.

Another week passed and once again, it was a Friday. I took a brief break to walk around the compound to get some exercise and clear my head. As I was nearing the office, an enormous boom shook everything! It seemed to cause the buildings to fold up and then return to their upright positions. What on earth could that be? The thought of the SPLA advance was never far from anyone's mind.

An army plane had dropped a load of fuel or a bomb; we didn't know which. It landed in an uninhabited area about a half mile from our compound. I didn't know whether to worry more about the SPLA or the army. Both were forces to be reckoned with, and I hoped not to have to be too close to either.

Love,

L

———————

Dear Harriet,

To live successfully in a country, it helps to like the local food. It turns out being from the southern part of the U.S. was a significant advantage. Why? I grew up eating okra, even the slimy kind. Okra forms one of the basic ingredients of many Sudanese dishes, along with garlic, onion, and tomato paste.

As you know, okra is best when picked early, when it is about the size of a man's little finger. If it gets much bigger, it becomes hard and inedible. In the U.S., I had only experienced the smooth variety—soft fur on the outside that washed off or disappeared in the cooking process. However, in Sudan, we have the sticky variety where the soft fur is more like a briar patch. Those briars burrow into my fingers while washing the okra and scratch my throat while I'm eating it. I guess the Sudanese don't enjoy having their throats scratched, so most women peel the ridges to eliminate some of the roughage.

I've eaten okra about every way there is to cook it, but fried is the most common way. Steamed okra on top of potatoes and green beans took a little longer for me to enjoy. It comes out soft and tasty without too much slime. The genuine test of an okra lover is to enjoy it boiled. Boiled okra is just plain slimy. Until I got to Sudan, the only people I ever met who liked slimy okra were real Southerners.

The Sudanese like the slime for one simple reason. Sudanese do not eat with forks as we do in the West. They eat with the right hand. The technique of eating with your right hand appeared to be straightforward, at least until I tried it. People use bread, *kisra*, or *asida* as a spoon. Ten-inch loaves of bread are two inches around and quite dense. *Kisra* is a large, thin crepe-like pancake that is folded over several times and tastes a bit sour. *Asida* is cornmeal put into boiling water, rather like thick, sticky grits. One takes the bread or whatever and dips it into a bowl of meat or vegetable sauce. If the sauce is too thin, it won't adhere to the bread or *kisra*. But by adding okra to the stew or sauce, the slimy quality helps the sauce cling to the bread and you get more of it to eat.

If a household runs out of okra, there is a backup plan. I bet you didn't know that okra could be dried and pounded into a powder that is called *weeka*. They can store the powder for use when okra is out of season. When the powder hits the boiling water, it makes the stew slimy.

Some Westerners frown on the practice of eating with your hand, but do you know who last used your fork or spoon? This method also saves on dishwashing, as each person washes his or her own hand at the end of the meal.

It seemed simple enough to eat with one's hand, but stains on my clothes from the drips of food say otherwise. The trick is to mold the *kisra*, bread, or *asida* into a flat semicircle within your four fingers. Dip that into the bowl. Then raise your hand to your mouth and push the food off your fingers with your thumb—right into your mouth. The Sudanese did it with a smooth, simple action. Proper etiquette says only the first knuckle should touch the food. If you get sauce higher on your fingers than that, it was clear you were not a very skilled eater and also had poor table manners. One Sudanese friend was trying to be helpful by showing me the proper way to pick up the *asida* and then dip it in the sauce. I thought I was copying exactly what he did, but he burst out laughing and said, "You eat like a monkey!" I expect I still do.

Love,

L

Dear Harriet,

Some days I envy you. There are two huge supermarkets where you can pick out any of a thousand things. You don't have to speak to anyone if you don't want to. When you leave, you can pay with cash, a check, a debit card, or a credit card. They bag up your groceries and you roll your shopping cart out to the car, put the bags inside, and drive home. What a life! I never knew buying food could be as challenging as it is in Juba.

Going to "the market" in Juba has a very different meaning. Depending on what you want to buy, you either go to a shop for packaged goods or to the open-air market for fruits, vegetables, or meat.

For example, I decided it would be nice to have something special to drink at my party. In Khartoum we used *asiir* (flavored sugar water). It came in several colors, purple for grape, orange for orange, red for, well, I'm not sure what the red tasted like. Except for the orange, they all tasted the same. Since this was a "packaged item," I went to several shops asking for it and was disappointed that none of them had any *asiir*. One shopkeeper explained it was "out of season." So, I made lime juice for the party.

The market area was full of shops standing side by side. Each one was approximately 12 x 12, with a counter across the front to prevent customers from going inside. Goods were stacked neatly on shelves from floor to ceiling on three sides of the shop. There might be a freezer or piles of boxes in the middle of the floor. The shopkeeper sat inside until he saw someone approach, then came to the counter to discover what the customer would like. It was difficult to see all the items in a shop, but since every shop contained the same things, once I figured it out, I knew what all of them had. Likewise, if one was out of some commodity, they were all without it.

While buying flour, I saw a printed notice on the flour sack: "Gift from the people of the United States of America. Not to be sold." I pointed out the notice to the shopkeeper, who was selling me flour from this sack. He explained the distribution would be better and fairer if sold in the shops. I guess the question was, fairer for whom?

Most shopkeepers were northerners, so we understood each other's Arabic pretty well. I never really learned the Arabic spoken in Juba, as it differed considerably from Khartoum Arabic. The traders enjoyed chatting with a foreign woman but asked more personal questions than I preferred. For example, one shopkeeper asked if I was married. When I told him, "No," he asked if I would marry him. The next time someone asked me if I was married, I said, "Yes." He asked, "Is your husband at home? If not, can I come to visit?" I convinced a male friend to wander around the market with me a time or two, so it looked as though I had a husband. So much for friendly conversation.

By far the most interesting part of the market, however, was the outdoor part. Men and women from outlying villages brought in their produce. The sellers displayed fruit or vegetable, spice, or handiwork on mats on the ground. If the person sold potatoes, for instance, the potatoes would be in small piles of maybe four to five. If I wanted potatoes, I said how many piles I wanted. Moving from one person to another, I would purchase green leaves from one, garlic from another, and tomatoes from a third. I picked the ladies to buy from so I didn't have to engage in discussions about my marital status. The women were often rather shy, and it was fun to be friendly with them. I expect it gave them plenty to gossip about after I had gone.

Prices in Juba were very low, and small change came in handy. It was hard to buy enough of anything to need paper money. If I needed to break a pound note and the vendor didn't have change, she would tell me to wait. Then she scurried around to other vendors to get the needed change. They never cheated me or failed to return with the right amount. If she couldn't find change, she gave me extra of whatever I was buying. Potatoes were the exception. Potatoes don't grow that far south but were flown in from Khartoum. That extra transportation made the potatoes pricey. But we willingly paid the price for the luxury of eating something familiar.

During certain times of the year, going to the market became a hardship. The first such occasion comes during the "hunger" time. Before the rains started, everyone ran out of food while waiting for the planting and harvesting. During that period, all I could find in the market were garlic and onions. We lived on canned goods or whatever we had stored in our freezer, or we did without. The other time was during mango season. Everyone had mangoes for sale. Piles of fist-sized mangoes lay ripening in the sun. They were picked ripe off the tree, and the longer they sat in the sun, the riper they became. The riper they became, the juicier and sweeter they became, and that drew flies to the sticky syrup that formed on the skin. Everyone ate mangoes and sucked on the large pit in the middle before throwing it on the ground. These mango stones attracted more flies. Soon, swarms of flies hovered over the ground until it was invisible because of the black cloud of flies.

I was not alone in my disgust of flies during mango season. Sister Theresa shared my feelings. She was in charge of the school grounds where she taught, and she threatened the children with severe punishments if they dropped mango pits or peels on the playground. She told me she had threatened anyone throwing a mango on the ground. She said she would put his right hand down the toilet and then make him wipe his face with it. I don't think she ever did that, but the children lived in fear that she might. Their schoolyard was spotless.

Love,

L

Dear Harriet,

The butcher's stall was the most dangerous place in the market. The Dinka or Mundari butchered meat on certain days. Enormous tree trunks placed on a concrete slab served as butcher blocks. A metal roof covered the area so work could continue, even if it rained or the sun was hot. They suspended the parts of the carcass that were available on large metal hooks. Green bottle flies buzzed everywhere and covered most of the meat. Poorer people only could afford the less desirable parts of the cow such as the tail or the feet. They wasted nothing. I purchased roast or something with no bones or sinew to cut away. It was difficult enough to get off the hard, dry chunks of fat.

To buy meat, I had to get close enough to the butcher to shout out what weight and cut of meat I wanted. I also tried to avoid being hit by flying bone chips. Sudanese stews have more bone than meat. The butcher chops up the bones, so that the marrow gets cooked into the sauce. Meals were more nourishing and more people got the benefit of the nutrients than if everyone had to have a chunk of meat. In our household, we took turns going for meat, as it was NO one's favorite job. We thought of becoming vegetarians, but it was hard to get enough protein in our diet as it was.

One of my colleagues who lived among the Murle in southeastern Sudan used to hunt a lot. When he arrived home from his hunt, everyone in the area would visit, hoping to get a share of the meat. In those days, rifles were rare, so locals appreciated Jon bringing in some game. It is always tricky in a foreign culture to share. Friends get offended if one doesn't do it according to local standards. After discussions with his good friend and cook, they agreed the cook would evaluate how much was available to be divided. He took a reasonable portion for the family. If there was meat left over, he divided out some for the circle of friends closest to Jon and his family. If meat were still available, he would divide out more for the next level of friendship and so on until it was all gone. That seemed to satisfy everyone, or at least everyone who mattered.

Our alternative to the meat market, while still having meat, at least occasionally, was to join a hunting party. Various men of our organization liked to hunt, but mileage costs on the group vehicles made it a rather expensive hobby. Therefore, they agreed to a request from our household to help pay the cost of the hunting trip if we took a share of the game they shot. They preferred we go with them, though I'm not sure how much Hillene or Cathy contributed. The hunters excused me from going because of my severe grass allergies. It was safer if I stayed home away from the high grass and just paid mileage for my share.

Sometimes they brought back nice things like dik dik or oribi. Both are small, tender antelopes. Sometimes they got a warthog. It was the only pork available, but tough as whang leather (whatever whang leather is!). On one occasion, they got a buffalo. Shooting a buffalo was a mixed blessing. It provided a great deal of meat if you could manage two things. First, it was not easy to get the carcass loaded onto the pickup. The buffalo didn't jump up into the pickup before it died. Once it was dead, it was heavy! Second, the meat had to be pressure-cooked a long time to get it tender enough to chew it. Ground buffalo was preferable.

Since they excused me from going on hunting trips, I got handed the delightful job of cutting up the meat when the gang arrived home about 8:00 pm. There's nothing like a 10 lb. chunk of buffalo meat complete with skin, fat, gristle, hair, and bone at 8:00 on a Saturday night to liven up your weekend!

Love,

L

Dear Harriet,

My thoughts have turned once again to food. Sister Theresa introduced me to a Shilluk family living in Juba. The wife's name was Priscilla and her husband was away working somewhere. She stayed in a government house in Juba with the children. It was fascinating to sit in their compound and watch the activities. Two of her girls sat under the shade of a large tree, one braiding the other's hair. The braider sat in a chair while the "braidee" sat on the ground in front of her. She sectioned the hair into tiny amounts and then braided it so tightly that it pulled the skin up off the skull. It took days to finish one head and must have caused a headache until the hair grew out a bit. They left the braiding in for weeks or months without taking it down. The hair's owner just washed the braids.

In another patch of shade, a woman was ironing clothes. She didn't use an ironing board, just a metal table. The charcoal iron looked heavy. The clothes needed to be dampened in order to get the wrinkles out and I watched in fascination as the woman took a sip of water out of a nearby cup and then sprayed the water through her teeth onto the area she was about to iron. It worked well, but I decided a spray bottle was a lot easier.

One afternoon during a visit, someone appeared with a kettle of tea and a tray of juice glasses. Sugar was measured into cups using a heaping teaspoon. Most Sudanese take three spoons of sugar in a fruit juice-sized glass of tea. The woman poured the boiling hot tea into the glasses and stirred vigorously. Then she brought my glass of tea on a tray. I realized, after I picked it up, that the glass was also boiling hot and I had no place to put it down to let it cool.

I quickly moved my fingers around from the top to the bottom to the side to here and there to keep from dropping the whole thing while my fingers sizzled. At last, someone saw my dilemma and brought over a small table so I could set down the glass. Once it cooled off, flies discovered the sugar syrup around the top and I had to brush them away and down my tea before they cheated me out of it.

I must have provided a certain amount of entertainment for the family as well, because they invited me over one day for a special Shilluk lunch. It was my first time to eat in a Shilluk home and I was eager to see what they ate. Mostly, the food was standard Sudanese fare, and most of the contents were identifiable. I enjoyed the meal and complimented my hostess on her culinary skills. When I took a second helping of one dish, she told me it was a Shilluk specialty. I inspected it more closely, because it looked like macaroni in tomato sauce. The macaroni was a little chewy, but otherwise I couldn't see anything unusual about it. Then Sister Theresa, who had joined us for the meal, told me the Shilluk name of the dish, *cin dyek*. I should have left well enough alone, but I had to let her tell me what that meant. Would you believe, sheep's intestines? That was NOT macaroni.

What do you do when you find yourself with a second helping of sheep's intestines in tomato sauce? Having professed that I liked it, I couldn't refuse to eat it. I forced my mind away from what it was and finished it. I have now learned to identify *komania*, the Arabic equivalent, and avoid it. Having said that, I did like the Shilluk version better, and best if I didn't know what it was.

Love,

L

Dear Harriet,

I bet you didn't know Juba had a soda factory. At home we call that a Coke factory because all fizzy soft drinks are "cokes." Anyway, the drinks produced in Juba were called Amit. I think that means "sweet thing." And they met that description: They were sweet and came in a variety of colors: orange, red, yellow, white, brown, and clear. We purchased them in glass bottles with a cap that you had to take off with a bottle opener. They sold drinks by the case or individually in most shops.

Since drinks were produced locally, the sodas were inexpensive, and I assume they used clean water because no one I knew ever got very sick from drinking them occasionally. I never got sick from them and I had the weakest stomach in Africa. One couple stayed about three months. The husband had a lot of stomach problems until we discovered that he was not drinking water because he feared it was not clean. Instead, he was only drinking Amit. We suggested he go back to water and his health improved. Otherwise, people just enjoyed them with no ill effects.

Mike, the local schoolteacher for the expatriate children, took the kids on a field trip to the Amit factory. It was an interesting trip, as the process for bottling this drink was distinctive. Since I missed getting to see this process myself, I asked Mike for his description and this is what he told me:

"Upon entering the compound, there were several 55-gallon fuel drums boiling over open fires, filled with returned Amit bottles. I suppose this was their cleaning and sterilization process. I remember watching the man fill the clean, empty bottles with the sweet syrup. The bottles were in cases on an assembly line. Equipped with a bucket of syrup, a measuring cup (about 1/3 cup size) and a little funnel, he quickly put the funnel into each bottle top and poured in the syrup.

"Next, the bottles went to the 'bottler.' There were several machines that filled a bottle with water, shot some carbon dioxide gas into it and then capped it. They were manual machines that dealt with one bottle at a time. The operator placed each bottle on the receptacle and pulled the lever down. Presto! One filled, gassed, and capped Amit drink bottle!

"For the last step, the bottles went to the quality control line. Several ladies sat at a long assembly line with long fluorescent light tubes shining in their faces from the back side of the table. They held the bottles up to the lights to check for anything that didn't belong; pieces of glass, bugs, dirt, who knows what else?

"The factory also had an ice-making machine that produced large blocks of ice. This seemed the biggest miracle to me in that hot, hot town. The ice was a separate product from the Amit drink but proved a useful 'extra' for stores."

Having heard how the drinks were made, most of us left a little soda at the bottom of the bottle for two reasons. One was the cultural cue that if you drained a glass to the bottom, it signaled to your hostess that you wanted more, so the hostess provided more water or tea or soda. Second, we hoped the heavier "floaty" things would settle to the bottom of the bottle, and it was best to leave them there.

Love,

L

———

Dear Harriet,

When people live in the wilder places of the world, today's topic comes around: toilets. We Americans shy away from that word, using any substitute we can think of: powder room, ladies'/men's room, bathroom, the "little" room, pit stop. But when it comes down to it, we choke rather than speak what it is. The British and most of the rest of the world are less squeamish. When you've experienced a few of the "less modernized" versions, it becomes a common topic of entertaining conversation. So, here you go.

There are two types of toilets: those designed to flush and those that aren't. Of those designed to flush, I found two types: those that do and those that don't. If they don't, it is a maintenance problem or a lack of water. This is the worst problem because it requires serious and unpleasant action on someone's part. When confronted with this situation, find a bucket of water and stand back while dumping the water into the too-full bowl.

Having tackled the worst-case scenario, we can now move on to less disgusting problems. We are still in the "flush" category. In Sudan, two styles are available: the sit-down and the footprint. The sit-down type is what we are most familiar with but was not always the optimal choice. The toilet seat might not be clean or indeed it may be missing altogether. If the toilet seat had a crack, it might pinch sensitive parts of the body. It is possible for a snake to coil up under it. This happened to my friend, Lynne. She sat down, squishing the unseen snake. The snake took offense and bit her in an unfortunate location. She survived the attack, but afterwards, lifted the seat to check before sitting down.

The footprint type offers two porcelain steps, one on each side of the hole. I've never been sure if it matters which way one stands. The water tank is above and has a pull chain to flush it. Good knees are very helpful.

Once you accomplish your purpose, you face the dilemma of "to flush or not to flush." If there is a water shortage, we use the motto: If it's yellow, let it mellow; when it's brown, flush it down.

Then you had to figure out how to flush it. Some water chambers supply a chain that you pull down, others include a handle that you press, still others have a string that you pull up. Some, as I've suggested, had a bucket of water nearby that you threw into the basin and hoped for the best.

By far my preference in most travel situations is the non-flushing variety or the long-drop. These toilets have a large hole, often twenty feet deep and eight to ten feet square, with a large cover, preferably of cement. A small hole provides access and guarantees you don't fall in. I've lost count of the number of items people have lost, from flashlights to guns. I've heard tales about people who fell or nearly fell in. Nightmares may occur if I think too much about it. But they required little cleaning, no water, and good knees. A few have seats.

The most unusual solution I've heard of or experienced in the toilet line was the bucket latrine. This alternative was a cross between the other two and was introduced by the British while they were governing Sudan. They constructed an outhouse near the outside wall of the compound. Inside was a platform with a hole. It might have a seat. Under the hole was a bucket. Once a week, the night crew came to collect the contents of the buckets. They lifted a small door in the wall, pulled the bucket out, emptied it into a wagon, and then replaced the bucket, more or less. Emptying the buckets provided jobs, done at night so as not to inconvenience the users, and allowed the workers to remain anonymous. The system worked but had the unfortunate side effect of attracting undesirable elements. My friend Anne told of the time she was crouched over a bucket trying to maintain her balance when a rat ran across her feet. I don't know about you, but I would have lost it. When I confirmed this story with her, she said the rat fell into the bucket and was still swimming for its life the next morning. I guess that doesn't bear thinking about anymore.

The ultimate challenge was where to go when there was no place to go. If there were bushes or large rocks, one could find a place for that "quiet moment." But in the desert, those things could be hard to find. So, my rule of thumb is to always carry toilet paper and a plastic bag and wear a very full skirt.

Love,

L

Dear Harriet,

I've mentioned guesthouses in my letters. Guesthouses offer cheaper accommodation for visiting employees, and a higher charge for guests from outside the organization supplies extra income. Guesthouse rates are considerably lower than a hotel.

The guesthouse in Juba had eight rooms, with a bathroom in between each pair of rooms. Additionally, there was a lounge and dining room with an adjoining kitchen. One problem with the room arrangement is when one person enters and locks the door but forgets to unlock it when they leave. Access becomes a challenge. Once, I stayed in room 2 and shared a bathroom and shower with the Sudanese man staying in room 1. It was not altogether satisfactory, as the Sudanese often squatted on the sit-down toilet seat.

Someone had decorated our guesthouse in a haphazard, leftover style, which meant that nothing matched. Most guests appreciated having a bed to sleep in, a roof over their heads, and a few meals provided. But then Lillie arrived. She was a black American who came to run the guesthouse for a year. Most importantly, she was an interior decorator.

During her first night in the guesthouse, she could not sleep because of the clashing colors. Even when the generator shut off, plunging the place into total darkness, the colors kept jarring her artistic sensibilities. She started planning her strategy on the spot.

Early in the morning, Lillie was sitting outside under a tree, making notes of the things she wanted to change. She had dressed in a lovely purple T-shirt and a pair of plaid shorts. She had a nice figure and in an American setting, would have been appropriately attired. But in Africa, the rules are different, especially for black women. I hurried over to greet her and suggested she change her clothes before too many people saw her. She didn't understand the problem until I explained that for a woman to wear shorts in Africa, revealing her legs, was equivalent to going topless in the U.S.

"Oh!" she cried. "I didn't know that!" She dashed to her room to put on a skirt. After that, she was careful how she appeared in public.

Within twenty-four hours of her arrival, she had been to the market and purchased material to make matching bedspreads and curtains. Within two weeks, there was a remarkable improvement in all the rooms. One of her final touches was to decorate the common sitting area. She purchased material for chair cushions that was navy, green, and cream striped. Next, she wanted the walls painted to complement the chairs. She instructed the painters to paint the wall green, with a six-inch strip of blue at the very top. Assured that they understood, she headed off to the market to take care of some shopping. When she returned, the painters were getting on well, painting the lower half of the wall green and the upper HALF blue.

"Stop! Stop!" she shouted at the painters. "That is not what I wanted!"

"But you will like it this way," they replied.

"No, I won't!" she countered. "Now do what I told you. The blue is only six inches from the ceiling and no farther!" She watched their every move to make sure they carried out her instructions.

That afternoon, I asked why she put the blue stripe on the top of the wall. Her reply? "Anyone can paint a wall green. It takes an interior decorator to put the stripe at the top!" And I guess that's right. I would never have thought of it.

The Africans interacted easily with Lillie. Her dark skin and curly black hair provided instant rapport with the Sudanese that my white skin and straight brown hair could never give. But the rapport came with a cost. She looked African, so they expected her to know the cultural rules and the language! I could break every rule of etiquette and mangle their language but would always be forgiven. I didn't look as if I belonged there. Lillie looked like an African, but when she didn't know the culture, the locals didn't understand it. Other black Americans have had a similar problem.

I remember hearing of one African American woman who worked in the north of Sudan. The locals expected her to wear a *tobe* and to keep her head covered whenever she was in public, no matter how hot it was. They became angry when they spoke to her and she didn't understand what they were saying. She had a harder time fitting into the society than a white woman, because the expectations for African Americans were so different.

Love,

L

———

Dear Harriet,

My T-shirt reads "I saw Halley's Comet from Juba, Sudan." Yes, that's where I was when the famous comet appeared in 1986. News announcers talked about it, even telling us how to find it. We got up at 4:00 a.m. to see if we could locate it. We had borrowed field glasses from the pilot. He had one pair of real field glasses and one pair of opera glasses. We took them both so each of us could study the sky.

The next morning, I crawled out of my comfortable waterbed and pulled on my clothes, a jacket, and a pair of shoes. Then I tapped on the adjoining wall to awaken Lillie. We stood in the middle of the compound, gazing at the sky. The trees blocked our view, and we were none too sure in which direction we should look. We moved out to the dirt road where nothing obstructed our view. We peered through the field glasses but didn't see a thing. Mornings are not my best time of day since I'm never fully awake until 9:00. After a few minutes, the early light of dawn appeared, and we realized not one star was visible in the overcast skies. We put the glasses away and went back to bed.

For the next few nights, one of us checked the weather. We didn't want to get up if it was rainy. At last, there was a clear night. We got up to try again. The stars shone brightly, but with the opera glasses, I saw only one or two stars at a time. We gave the opera glasses back to Denny. Meanwhile, we didn't know which of these lights in the sky was the comet. Our Sudanese guard came to inquire why we were up at that early hour. We explained in local Arabic that we were looking for the comet. "Oh," he said, "it's right over there!" He watched the stars every night and knew what was normally there. He had noticed the comet immediately. We bragged to our friends that we had seen Halley's Comet.

After that, everyone else wanted to view it, but didn't want to bother unless it was visible. So, they asked us to act as the early morning spotters. If the sky was clear, we should get everyone up for a look. The schoolteacher, Mike, arranged for the school children to sleep overnight in the *tukul* where we held our meetings. They got up early to spot the comet and eat cinnamon rolls. Lillie and I felt cheated that we didn't get any cinnamon rolls!

Several weeks later, other single expats decided to take a photograph of the comet. It was one of those challenges: "Get YOUR photo of Halley's Comet in YOUR local paper." The Nile Monitor didn't have many people vying for that distinction. By that time, the comet became visible in the early evening around 9:00 p.m. Six of us stood in the middle of the compound, studying the sky to locate the comet. It was nowhere to be seen. We had decided we had lost it when the guard came over to ask what we were doing. We explained we were looking for the comet.

"Oh," he said with a sigh, "it's over there now." He pointed in the opposite direction, and sure enough, there it was. We experimented with our cameras, leaving the shutter open for varying numbers of seconds. The only thing that showed up in our photos was the black sky. But, with a bit of help from the guard, we can claim to have seen Halley's Comet twice.

Love,

L

———

Dear Harriet,

My goal during this research year was to get accurate data on the Shilluk verbs, vowels, tones and nouns. I don't think I'm exaggerating when I say that Shilluk ranks right up there with Mandarin Chinese and classical Arabic as being one of the world's most difficult languages. For years I just thought I was slow, but I realized that while I might be inexperienced and somewhat disorganized, the inescapable fact was the Shilluk language was unusually complicated.

Sister Theresa helped me when available, but her job required her to travel outside Juba. She got me in touch with other Shilluk speakers and that was helpful. Among them was Mark, a meteorologist at the airport. He helped find the names of animals and plants that Sister Theresa didn't know. While working with him, I realized how different vocabularies were for men and women. Men learned the names of cow colors and wild animals, while women knew color words for beads, the names of pots and dishes, and household related words. Women rarely allow men into the kitchen, so that vocabulary is unknown to them.

One evening, I came for my lesson and discovered Mark was packing to leave that night for Saudi Arabia. They offered him a job, and he had to leave immediately. (No one in his right mind turns down a job in Saudi.) He apologized he couldn't help me anymore, but he had written out a list of words for me, all in Shilluk. I asked, "How can I find out what the words mean?" He sent me to work with John. They went to primary school together and learned to read Shilluk at the same time.

One Tuesday evening, I turned up at John's house for my lesson. I showed him Mark's list of words, but he wasn't able to read it. This was symptomatic of the problem with the Shilluk writing system: It wasn't readable by anyone other than the person who wrote it. I might guess at a word, but my pronunciation was poor. I'm sure it hurt their ears to hear me mangle their language with the wrong tones, vowels, vowel and consonant length, and voice quality. The problem was that THEY couldn't read it. There wasn't enough information written to tell them what the words meant, especially out of context.

Since identifying the meanings of the words on the list wasn't getting us anywhere, I tackled the problem from a different angle. I asked John to name different colors of things: the red tablecloth, the blue of the wall, the white shirt. This exercise clearly bored him.

Then I remembered that Shilluk men love to talk about their cows. I pulled out the embroidery threads I carried with me. I had thirty different shades of color, from white to black, represented. "Do you have cows the color of these threads?" I asked. John's eyes lit up, and he said, "Oh, yes! We have names for all those colors for cows." He named every one of them, including three more shades of yellow, four shades of orange, five shades of red, several shades of blue, green, and purple besides the multiple browns, blacks, and grays. "And in between these two colors we have ..." and so it continued—forever! I did not know what color names to write because there were so many. Next, he described the shapes of the colors on the cow: streaked, spotted, and striped. When he ran out of those, he described other features. There was the black cow with the white spot on its tail, the white cow with one black foot, the brown cow with the white streak on its face, and on and on and on. Next, he moved on to the shapes of the horns. Shilluks shave the horns on their long-horned cattle to make them go in interesting directions. There are the two horns pointing forward, or the right horn forward and the left horn to the back. Both horns may go straight up or curve downward to the side. They may form a heart shape over the head or a Greek lyre with the tips pointing up and away from each other. That list continued on and on as well. I left after three hours with my head spinning and my dreams filled with cattle of every conceivable size, shape, and color.

Love,

L

Dear Harriet,

In searching for Shilluks, I found a few who worked at the University of Juba. The Dean of Students, Arop, was away in Khartoum most of the time, but eventually I met him and his wife, Arek. We became very close friends when all of us moved to Khartoum. A geology professor offered to help me. His name was Dr. Peter, but most people called him Komorade (Comrade). He studied for his degree in Yugoslavia during communist rule, so when he returned to Sudan, his nickname became "Comrade." As a geologist, he had analyzed the soil the large digger at the Sobat site had to dig through to create the canal. A video program documenting the canal project described the difficulties involved. The narrator pointed out that the composition of the soil was proving to be a challenge, as it was not what they expected.

In Budapest, Komorade found a book from 1902 about the Shilluk language. He made a photocopy and bound it in two volumes. When he learned of my interest in the language, he loaned them to me. I didn't know why he left the books in my keeping. Within a few months, he disappeared from town and joined the SPLA. I understand he later became a commander and lost a leg in the fighting.

Time was running out, and I didn't have the information I needed. No one had hours to work with me because they had jobs. Then I heard of a Shilluk family living in Kenya. The husband, Peter, was on a break from his college studies. He and his wife, Rachel, agreed to my coming to Kenya to work with them for a month. This was the break I needed. So, in April 1986, Peter and I worked three to four hours a day exploring the Shilluk language. He whistled tones and read lists of words to compare vowels and thought of sentences using as many verbs as we could think of. Shilluk has a verb for everything you can imagine and many you can't imagine. The puzzle started falling into place.

One day, Peter looked depressed and grumpy. When I asked what was wrong, he replied, "I haven't seen the sun for three days." It had been cloudy and rainy, but I hadn't noticed. Sudanese depend on the sun and miss it when it is hiding. I explained that in Britain I might not see the sun for a week. He didn't understand why anyone wanted to live in such a place. No wonder people in the north became depressed in the winter.

Thanks to my time with Peter, I understood more about the language and the changes needed to be readable by the Shilluks. Upon returning to Juba, the news on the war-front continued to worsen; it felt more tense every day. I decided if I couldn't stand the heat, I'd better get out of the kitchen.

So, I packed up my house one more time and stored my worldly goods in the warehouse. I got on a plane and returned to London to continue my studies for my Ph.D. The hardest part of leaving a country at war is not knowing what will happen to one's friends. The Sudanese weren't able to fly away as I had.

Love,

L

———————

Dear Harriet,

All this dislocation and working with many different Shilluk speakers had a positive result. If I had analyzed the language with just two or three people, I would make my assumptions and they would probably affirm my findings. However, when I changed speakers, they challenged my incorrect analyses, and I had to change them. With each change, I got closer to the right answer.

My original proposal was to describe the grammar of Shilluk. But it soon became clear that if I didn't understand the sound system, I couldn't begin to analyze the grammar. So, in 1988, I completed my dissertation/thesis: *An Autosegmental Approach to Phonological Phenomena in Shilluk*. I typed the whole thing on a Sharp almost-computer with an eight-line screen using dot commands. I think the Sharp had a 48k memory bubble, as that was all one would need on a computer.

My supervisor, Dick, said he could spend only eight hours each week reading my dissertation. I wanted to finish by August so I could spend some time at home with my parents before returning to Africa. I began to pray earnestly that Dick would finish reading what I had written.

I saw Dick early the next week, and he handed back my work. "I finished reading it," he said. He had traveled by train to Wales on Friday, and the train broke down for hours. The only thing he had with him was my dissertation. When he realized that, he thought to himself, *Leoma has been praying again!*

During my final year in England, I received a letter from the Sudan director asking where I wanted the things I had left in Juba. Everyone was evacuating. Should my things go to Nairobi or to Khartoum? The Shilluk area was much closer to the north, and if people were going to flee, they would go to Khartoum. And with that, the next stage of my adventure became clear.

Love,

Dr. L

Glossary of Foreign Words

Arabic words

Allah yibarak fiik—may God bless you

Allah yisallimak—may God bring you peace

Al hamdu li'llah—God be praised

Angareb—a bed with a wooden or metal frame and rope or plastic string as the bed

Arbaiin—40th street

Arda—street name

Asida—a thick cornmeal mush

Asiir—flavored drink mix in a liquid form

Banbur—small footstool

Bika—wake for a funeral

Bukra—tomorrow

Dabiib—snake

Eilba—tin can

Fii—there is

Habbouba—grandmother

Habuub—dust storm

Haraka—fire

Hoosh—yard

Insha'allah—God willing, maybe

Itfaddal—permission to do whatever you would like or need to do

Jabal—hill or mountain

Jallabiya—a cotton garment rather like a dress. White is worn by men, but women also wear them but with lots of different colors. They can be thought of as Arab robes.

Kanoon—a square charcoal stove

Khawaja—foreigner

Kisra—a thin pancake often eaten with a stew

Komania—a savory dish of intestines

Ma'alesh—sorry, too bad

Mumtaz—excellent

Nahar—nose

Raajil maa fii—there are no men

Salaam aleekum—peace be with you

Sitta biyuut—six houses

Suuq—market

Taraha—a taxi shared with 3 others that goes on a set route

Tahnia—rather like sweet peanut butter made with sesame

Taskara—ticket

Tawiil—long, tall

Tobe—approximately six yards of material that women wrap around themselves to display modesty

Tukul—round mud hut with thatched roof

Tusker—a brand of beer

Weeka—okra that is dried and pounded into a powder

Zeer—unglazed ceramic pot for cooling water

British words

Biscuits—cookies

Chuffed—very pleased

Garden—yard

Loo—toilet

Lorry—truck

Petrol—gasoline

Sisters—nurses

Tea—usually a drink, but in other situations, an early supper for children

French/Cameroonian words

Baton d'manioc—stick of fermented cassava paste
Bilhartzia—Schistosomiasis, also known as bilharzia, is a disease caused by parasitic worms. (www.cdc.gov)
Filaria—a disease called river blindness, carried by large flies that bite
Jiggers—insects that burrow into toes and lay eggs
Panya or pagnes—six yards of material

Swahili words

Harami—thief
Kanga—brightly printed cotton cloth about the size of a single bed sheet
Kipilefti—roundabout
Matatu—van or pickup truck with a roof used for public transport
Panga—slasher, an 18" long blade with a curve at the end for slashing grass
Pole—sorry
Pole pole—slowly

Shilluk words

Aduung—type of lyre, musical instrument
Cin dyek—sheep intestines
Lawø—a cloth wrapped around the body and tied on one shoulder
Suud—swamp
Suuq aswad—black market
Thay wic—Shilluk facial markings

Other unfamiliar terms

Anya Nya—The rebel movement in south Sudan. The name comes from a poison used by the Ma'di language group.
Kokoro—separation; a demand for Nilotics to return to their own states and out of Juba

Leoma Gilley

Leoma was born and raised in Chattanooga, TN, as an only child. Her father was a gifted storyteller, and she inherited that gift and continues to develop it. She obtained her BS in speech and language pathology from the University of Tennessee and worked for several years as a speech therapist. She then studied for her MA in the same field and worked in a speech and hearing clinic in Macon, GA. In 1988, she earned a PhD in Linguistics from the University of London, School of Oriental and African Studies.

Linguistics fascinated Leoma, and in 1979 she felt called to join Wycliffe Bible Translators and SIL International. This affiliation led her to more adventure than she had expected and she lived most of her adult life in Africa, about twenty years of that in the Sudan. She has traveled widely and enjoyed discovering the languages and cultures of the places she visited. After thirty-seven years, she retired and settled in Knoxville, TN.

For more great books from the Peak Press
Visit Books.GracePointPublishing.com

PEAK PRESS

If you enjoyed reading *Launching into the Unknown,* and purchased it through an online retailer, please return to the site and write a review to help others find the book.